County Maps and Histories Series
Berkshire

Valerie G. Scott
and
Eve McLaughlin

Quiller Press

Published in Association with
Knight Frank & Rutley

The county maps and history of
Berkshire

*A*ntique maps are an ideal medium through which to view history. They show the changing landscape, the different social patterns of the period in which they were made, the coming of the canals and railways which had such a significant effect on people's lives, and the country homes of the rich and famous. The continuing fascination of an old map is that the more you study it the more information it reveals. In other words, to love old maps is to love history and vice versa.

Robert Louis Stevenson summed this up in *Treasure Island* when he said, 'I am told that there are people who do not care for maps, and find it hard to believe. The names, the shapes . . . the courses of the roads and rivers . . . are an inexhaustible fund of interest for any man with eyes to see or two-penceworth of imagination to understand with.'

It is surprising that in the past old maps have not been used more by historians. In this book on Berkshire, which is the second of a comprehensive series on the counties of Great Britain, we hope to right the balance by combining history and maps. By doing this we follow in the footsteps of the very early mapmakers many of whom systematically surveyed—often in appallingly difficult circumstances—and drew up maps of every county and then collated them into atlases. The antique maps, which we illustrate here, are taken from some of the most beautiful originals in existence. They come from collections in map libraries, in private hands, and in antique map galleries, and gratitude must go to those who have allowed us to handle and photograph their material.

The Royal County of Berkshire, with Windsor Castle as perhaps its most famous landmark, has had a chequered history with periods of great wealth and periods of depression. It is a most attractive county with a wide variety of scenery ranging from chalk downlands to rich pasture. Its position as a thoroughfare and a home for royalty and nobility has helped to shape its character.

From earliest times it has contained important routes like the ancient Ridge Way across the Downs, the Roman road from London to Silchester (known locally as the Devil's Highway) and later the main roads to Bath and Oxford. Perhaps most important for the transporting of goods in earlier times was old Grandfather Thames himself. His presence was vital although he could prove bad tempered in winter, when he brought storms and floods, and churlish in summer, when he let the water level drop too low, stranding the barges. The building of the canals and railways around the 1800s continued the trend leading up to today when the mighty M4 motorway slices through the county on its journey west. One of the reasons for this tradition of good communication, apart from Berkshire's geographical location, is the fact that it is one of the most level counties in England. The highest point does not reach 1,000 feet above sea level.

The boundary re-organisation of 1974 has brought great changes. A large chunk of land along the bank of the Thames has defected to Oxfordshire and means that Berkshire can no longer claim to be the only county with a bank of the River Thames along the whole of one of its sides. However, on the plus side (if it *is* a plus!) Berkshire has won Eton and Slough, which were previously in Buckinghamshire. There are great sporting traditions in the area including fishing, fox hunting,

hare coursing (the Royal Buckhounds were only abolished in 1901), horse racing at Ascot and even cockfighting. Ascot was a great occasion for cockfighting. In 1798 the *Reading Mercury* stated that 'during Ascot Races will be the great main of cocks . . . between the gentlemen of Kent and Sussex, for 5 guineas a battle and fifty the odd'.

There has been no great industry in the county apart from cloth making in the seventeenth century, founded on the excellent sheep pastures, and brick and pottery kilns. The earliest recorded industry was bell founding at Wokingham in the fourteenth century.

The first map to treat Berkshire as a separate county appeared in 1607. It was by William Camden, who was head-master of Westminster School, and mentions the Atrebates who were a tribe of people around before the Romans. These maps were engraved from the earlier survey by the Yorkshireman, Christopher Saxton (c. 1542–1610) one of the most important map-makers of all time and the first person ever to put together an atlas of the English Counties.

County Origins

The old County of Berkshire is shaped rather like an old boot—not an elegant piece of footwear suitable for strolling around the Royal Enclosure, or even a smooth green welly appropriate to the tax-loss farmyard, but a mashed, crushed object of hard old leather, which looks for all the world as if it has been dug out of some ancient and not particularly distinguished tomb. The 1974 boundary changes, which carved a lump off the top of the boot for Oxford, and patched on a bit of Bucks at the toe end, were obviously an attempt to pretty up the battered old shape, but no amount of slimming and trimming can alter the venerable age of the article.

Berkshire had no name until Alfred set up administrative counties in about 886. The often quoted notion that the name is 'from Berroc wood, so named because the box tree grows there' is based on one of the many errors in the copy of a copy of the lost *Life of Alfred* by the monk Asser, which also has him born at 'Wanating'. There is no Anglo-Saxon word *berroc* meaning box or anything else, to be found in Bosworth and Toller's definitive dictionary. Box is a low-growing, slow-growing shrub, scarcely visible in the thick forests of the time. The tall birch tree (beorc) abounded and was used for simple boats, general building, roofing shingles, utensil making, brooms and rods for punishment. Its bark was used in tannery and could be peeled thinly enough to make primitive notepaper. When Alfred wanted a name, he had only to look about him for these useful trees.

Berkshire was a busy place back in prehistoric times, or part of it was. The county is divided, like Gaul, into three parts: the northern tree-covered Vale of the White Horse, the southern smaller Vale of Kennet, with its heath and dense woodlands, and between them, the high Downs, solidly built of chalk, with an ancient path, the Ridge Way, running east to west. It was here that the prehistoric tribes lived and moved, not in the dangerous wet woods, where the wolf and bear roamed free. Up on the Downs are the earthworks which surrounded the little camps of the Beaker Folk, of Bronze Age men and Iron Age men. There too are their tombs, the round or long barrows

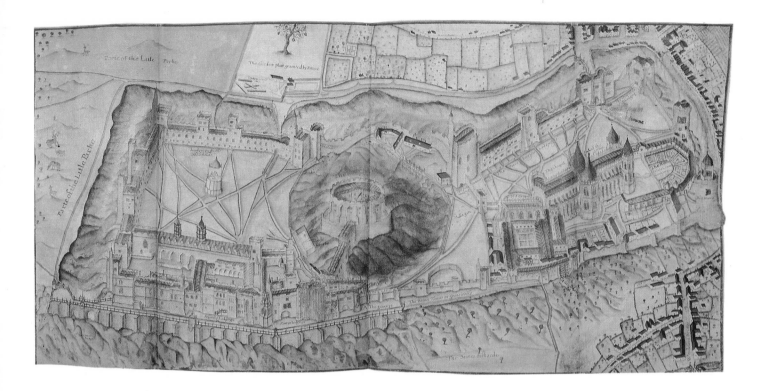

Windsor Castle by John Norden, 1607

John Norden's survey of Windsor Great Park opens with this magnificent bird's-eye view of the Castle "taken and performed by the perambulation view and delineation of John Norden in Anno 1607", and is followed by sixteen plans of the Park, showing the "walkes" and numbering the deer in each section. The book, finely bound and emblazoned with the Royal coat-of-arms, was presented to King James I who rewarded Norden with £200.

The Castle and Forest came into Royal possession under William the Conqueror. Norden's view records various periods of building: in the centre are the Norman gateway and the twelfth century Round Tower, though much of the building dates from the reign of Edward III in the fourteenth century. The most striking addition was Tudor —St George's Chapel at the right. Clearly, Norden's view is from his own observation, for he shows the numerous minor buildings inside the walls, wells, gardens and a real tennis court, complete with racquets.

As with most early surveyors, John Norden (1548–c.1625) depended on patronage and, at several critical points in his career, he presented gifts to win favour. He began mapping estates in 1588 in Northamptonshire, but planned a far more ambitious scheme—his Speculum Britanniae. He wanted to improve on the atlas of his contemporary, Christopher Saxton, by making new surveys of the individual counties and adding historical descriptions. After presenting his Northamptonshire map to Lord Burghley and a manuscript history to Queen Elizabeth I, he did win some support at Court but, in 1599, fell out of favour and his Speculum foundered. Eight counties were surveyed, but only two published in his lifetime. Under James I, Norden's fortunes improved and he was appointed Surveyor of the Lands of the Duchy of Cornwall. However, until his death, he limited his work to drawing estates and never revived his plans for a national survey. (MS Harl.3749, tab.I, by courtesy of the British Library)

where the casualties of natural diseases or local battles lie—and where the occasional warped and battered shoe, archetype of the county, is dug up.

There were Bronze Age settlements near Wallingford and Yattendon, where tools and weapons were stockpiled against the future need which passed too suddenly to use them. The little settlements, always in a state of preparation for attack, by animals or men, are known by military names—Badbury Camp, Walbury Camp, Uffington Castle, Letcombe Castle, Blewburton Camp, White Horse Hill Camp, all were once home to our remotest ancestors. Badbury was the great metropolis, with around sixty little pit dwellings while Uffington had a certain cachet as a defensible stronghold. It was there that a kind of primitive military museum was built up over the centuries, with the great sprawling figure of the White Horse as a sign. Traditionally, it was said to have been cut there by Alfred to celebrate his victory at Aescendun, but there is quite a possibility that it, or something like it, was there long before, and Alfred merely had it improved or extended. Contemporary accounts in his own time do not mention any large scale work of this kind after the battle.

One quite plausible theory about the White Horse is that it was originally a dragon, the ancient British badge, possibly cut to commemorate the burial nearby of the Pen-dragon, or chief of

all the Kings, and that it was converted to a horse later, when this became the rallying badge. Certainly, the shaping of the head is odd, and the outline of the body lacks the skill of Munnings or Stubbs, but they didn't have to chip out trenches a couple of feet deep in the stubborn chalk, or work to the scale of this great animal, about 370 feet long. The whole thing cried out for some supervisor in a helicopter, shouting 'Left hand down a bit' at intervals.

On the High Downs, it is still possible to get away from it all, to stand inside some earthwork, peering out across country, imagining the way our ancestors lived, affected by a terror of the approach of any stranger. Indeed, if another party of visitors dare follow, you feel as defensive of your earthwork as ever did Bronze Age man.

Opposite the White Horse is its Manger, a depression in the hillside which may have been the site of ritual fires. Along the Ridgeway is Wayland's Smithy, really a barrow with its central burial chamber uncovered. Wayland, elsewhere the maker of Heroes' Armour and magic swords, guaranteed to bring victory, is here domesticated as a farrier, handy for the military centre once at Uffington (and later the racehorses in which the county abounds). If you left a penny (or later sixpence) on a stone by the Smithy, Wayland must shoe your horse overnight. This seems an excellent chance for gangs of horse thieves to steal the bloodstock of the gullible.

The Belgic tribes who came later started to clear back the forests from the banks of the many small rivers of the area. This was hard work, and some settled for the less fertile terraces of soil cut into the sides of the downs—the 'lynchetts' still seen in places. The ruling tribe, the Atrebates, had their capital at Silchester (Calleva Atrebatum) and came to regard the present course of the Thames as their northern boundary. To watch for northern enemies, a small garrison was set on the Sinodun Hills, twin projections opposite Dorchester. From below, the twin hills with pallisaded towers reminded the earthier soldiery of the girls they left behind them—hence the alternative name of the 'Berkshire Bubs'.

The Ridgeway was part of the trading road of the Iceni, the Icknield Way from Norfolk to Cornwall. High paths meant safety and were very viable for most of the year, when the valleys were soaked and marshy. When the Romans came, their lines of communication were different, and their major road through Berkshire ran through Calleva, north-west along the Kennet towards Aquae Sulis (Bath). It was a holiday road, not an important military artery, though it passed Cirencester. Parts are still there, known as Ermine Street, but much of the Berkshire section is minor, and great lengths have been dug up long since. Near Broadmoor, the path was romantically christened the 'Devil's Highway', very much later.

The Romans also built minor lengths of roads to serve their villas, for they found Berkshire pleasant to live in. There was also a short military road, which linked Dorchester camp with the Sinodun Hills—the Romans recognised a good lookout position when they saw one. They also made use of the Ridgeway, which was straight(ish) and avoided marshy land. However, the bracing breezes of the Downs afflicted the thinner blooded southerners and they soon moved their trackway a mile or so down the side of the hill and built Portway, which runs past the Hendreds and Wantage, skirting Pendragon Hill instead of touching Uffington. One Roman built his villa under

Berkshire by William Kip
after Christopher Saxton, 1607

The first map to treat Berkshire as a separate county appeared in William Camden's Britannia. Camden (1551–1623), headmaster of Westminster School, first published his history of Britain in 1586 without maps, but, in all editions from 1607, maps were included to help the reader. The title of the Berkshire map shows its antiquarian scource. "Olim sedes Atrebatum" refers to the Atrebates who lived in the region before the Romans.

The maps in the 1607 Britannia were engraved from earlier surveys—mostly by the Yorkshireman Christopher Saxton (c.1542–1610/11). Berkshire is taken from his combined map of Oxfordshire, Buckinghamshire and Berkshire which he surveyed about 1574. Therefore, although the map reproduced here is from a 1610 edition of Camden's book, it shows the county as it was during the reign of Elizabeth I. No roads are included, but the all-important river crossings are marked. "Mole-hills" and bushy trees give only the vaguest impression of the Eastern Downs and woodlands which were so important to a thriving timber trade. Oddly, parts of Wiltshire appear in the county. This anomaly, due to an ancient gift of land, survived well into the nineteenth century.

Though Saxton's maps may not be accurate to modern eyes, his achievement was extraordinary. He had the fortune to win the patronage of Thomas Seckford, Master of Requests to Elizabeth I, and was able to complete the first national survey of England and Wales between 1570 and 1579. The practical and physical problems he faced are still not fully known but in 1579, Saxton published his atlas containing a general map and thirty four maps of the counties. The Queen rewarded him with a grant of land and a coat-of-arms. No one attempted a fresh survey of the whole of England until the nineteenth century and Saxton's maps were repeated again and again by all the leading mapmakers of the seventeenth century. (By courtesy of the Bodleian Library)

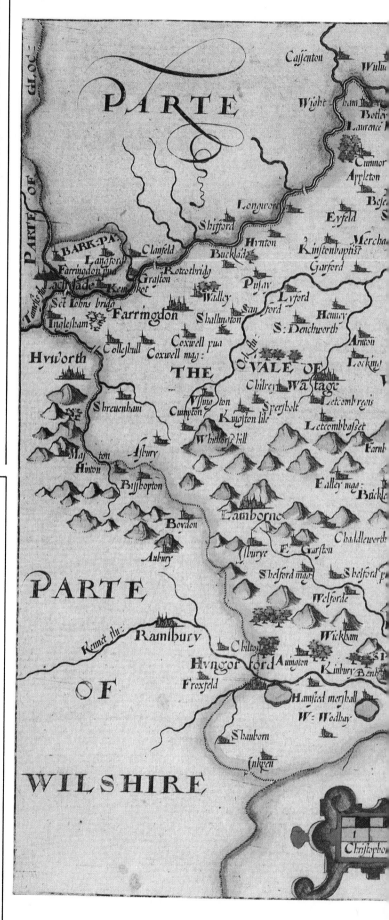

COMITATUS
Bercheriæ vulgo Bark-
shyre qui olim sedes A=
TREBATVM

PARTE OF

OF
OXFORD
Cowley
Iley
Kennington   Sanford
Radley
Abbington   Neuncham
Clyfton

OXFORD.

BVCK-

ING-   HAM

Barton   Lon: Iwinham   Dor sesten
Myston   Warboro
Apleford   Witham pua   Cranmershe   SHIRE
Sutton courtney   Brightwell   GALLENA   Bensington
Didcote   Wallingford   Nuncham
N: Morton   N: Stoke
S: Morton   Chonsey
Haborn   Aston   Ipsden
HORS   Blubery   Moulsford   Stoke
Chilton   Woodcote
Lhamsley hill   Coring   Whichurch
W: Isley   Streler
E: Isley   Cumpton   Aldworth   Bassilden   Pang born
Biddon   Ashamsted   Tilcherst
Hamsted   Lulmershe
rc   Nattington   Stanford   Suckham   Reding
Orwe chap: Frisham   Bradfeld
Cheneley   Bucklebury   Ingelsford   Thele
terborn   Bennehain   Osten   Burseld
Skan   Wolhampton   Padworth   Silhamsteds
Thatcham   Aldermerton   Stratfeld mortinere
rene   Kennet flu: Brymton   Wasna
Newberye   Anborne flu: Silchester   VINDONVM
Knight brida   Eadlow
Newtowne

Medenham   Merlow yng   Hedsor
Greneland   Merlow mag: Tames flu:
Hurley   Bysham   SHIRE
Remneham   Madenhead   Topley
Henley   Braye   Eaton Vpton   Datchet
Horspenden als harding   Waraune twisforde   Shatbrok   Dorney   Clure
Shiplake   Lawrente waltham   Withwaltham   Windsor
Cauersham   Ruscombe   The forest of   Old Winsor
Sunnynge   Windsor   The great plot of windsor
WILT-PARS   Billingesbere
Purley   Hurst   Binfeld   Winkfeld
Lod: bridg   Warfeld   Sunnynghill
Whity pk   Okingham
Arberfeld   Yatehamstead
Shinfeld   Barkham   Bagshot
Swalofeld   Finchamstead
WILT-PARS   Sandherst   Wingham
Hetfeld   Euersley   Yately   Blakwater   PARTE
Purges   OF   SVR:

PARTE OF

HAMSHIRE

REY

5   10

n descripsit .   Gulielmus Hole sculpsit

V

the shadow of the White Horse hill. It was a peaceful occupation here, and the locals shrugged and accepted their new neighbours.

Far more worrying were the Saxons, when they too invaded. The first onslaught of sea-borne raiders hit the coastal areas, but small boats brought them up the river. Soon, the Saxons settled at Cookham, Caversham and even Wittenham, after a bloody battle under the Sinodun Hills. But the main invasion came from the south and soon the Kennet Valley was settled and the Saxons took over Portway. The Romano-Britons extended the hand of cautious friendship and the Saxons felt so safe that their local Wessex chiefs brought up their children here.

In 636, King Cwichelm died and was buried at 'Cwichelm's Law' (Cuckhamsley) henceforth a place of veneration. His son, Cuthred, was too young to succeed, in these martial times, but his uncle, King Cenwalh, gave him 'three thousand hides at Aescendun' in 648. This was the name for the Ridgeway and the lands on either side of it—so effectively, he was the first to own the county of Berkshire as a unit.

The kingship passed to and fro among the descendants of Cerdic, always to an adult, since they were always fighting—even against the Mercians, the British, and their own cousins seeking the throne. At last, these kings of Wessex became almost hereditary Bretwaldas, or High Kings, over the country, after Egbert of Wessex was elected in 828. But almost at once, there was another threat, from sea-borne invaders, this time, the Danes or Northmen.

Every summer there was a raid, but the Danes did not settle until the overconfident King Ethelwulf went off to Rome for a year in 855, taking his youngest boy, Alfred, who was born in Wantage in 849. In 860, the men of Berkshire, under their ealdorman, came to the rescue of Winchester attacked by the 'pirates' and won a notable victory. In 868, it was time for Alfred to leave his studies, and join the last big brother, Ethelred, against the Danes. The struggle was desperate now, since the invaders had taken over almost the whole north and midlands and only Wessex remained. In 870, the final struggle began with a Danish attack on Reading and their advance west was stopped by the valiant ealdorman at Englefield. Chased back to Reading, the Danes fought a pitched battle there with the two princes, and won, with great losses on both sides. The princes retreated west to their home ground, the high Downs, and the Danes caught up with them at 'Aescendun', the same territory given to Cuthred.

For some reason, controversy reigns over the exact site of Aescendun. Tradition claims Ashdown or Ashbury and pinpoints 'Alfred's Camp' as north-west of the White Horse. Although the total area covered must have been wider, the general location sounds reasonable enough. Alfred grew up in Wantage, and knew how many earthworks there were in the hills above. He and his brother needed a defensive position fast—and if you stand on the Ridgeway at this point, you will appreciate the tactical possibilities.

Alfred won a famous victory, with heavy losses on the Danish side. However, there was no time to sit back and cut victory symbols, since within a fortnight, fresh Danish troops had poured into the south, and Alfred and Ethelred were badly defeated at Basing. For eight years afterwards, Alfred, by now sole King, was on the run and almost lost everything when he was driven into hiding in the Athelney marshes. Only in 877 did Alfred achieve a decisive victory and convert (or at least, baptise) the Danish leader. The real relief came when the Danes went off to raid France, where the King was much weaker, though they kept their hand in with summer raids. England was never totally free of them, but at least Alfred had the upper hand, except in Northumbria and East Anglia, which remained Danish.

There was no justification, or time, for cutting a victory horse in 870, after Aescendun, but perhaps in 877, the locals may have decided to clean up an existing one on the battle site. Alfred was their local boy and the Horse may have been the symbol of resistance, like the Cross of Lorraine in World War II.

For a few decades, Berkshire escaped the main force of battles. The Danes took over part of France, called Nor(th)mandy and settled down cosily. The Saxons expanded their settlements and

set up an integrated system of government, dividing the country into shires under an ealdorman, and a shire reeve or sheriff.

Then a new wave of Northmen appeared, anxious for the rich pickings of the west. Normandy was too tough for them, so they spent their holidays on a spot of rape and pillage in England. Again, the coast felt the first shock and the first settlements were made in Northumbria and Mercia. Wessex, including Berkshire, was safe from harm until King Edward was murdered by his wicked stepmother in 978, and her son, Ethelred, replaced him, in the absence of an adult male prince of the line.

Even when he grew up, Ethelred was an unmitigated disaster —his nickname 'Unready' means he was badly advised or incapable of accepting advice. Until his time, the Bretwalda was the focus of loyal support against the Danes, but Ethelred was so incompetent, ill-tempered and treacherous that his own ealdormen turned against him and his people thought there wasn't much to chose between their king and the Danes, except the Danes were rougher, tougher and *there*. Half the time Ethelred was skulking in the north-west when his people were under attack.

Danish raids penetrated even deeper and only their nomadic habit took them away from what were practically settlements. They wandered at will through the country, including up the Thames. Reading became a base where Ivar the Dane kept stores exacted from the local people. In 1005, a famine kept even the Danes away, but when they returned, they were so furious at finding the cupboard bare that they burnt Reading and Wallingford and even dared what a superstition had previously prevented, and set foot on the Ridgeway at Cwichelm's Tomb. The folk tale said that if they did, they would never reach the coast again. They came, sneered, beat the local levies and continued down to the coast, just to ram it home.

This superstition about Cwichelm's Law may be because it was the council place of Wessex, a sacred place which must be protected by the spirits of the old Kings. If so, they were asleep,

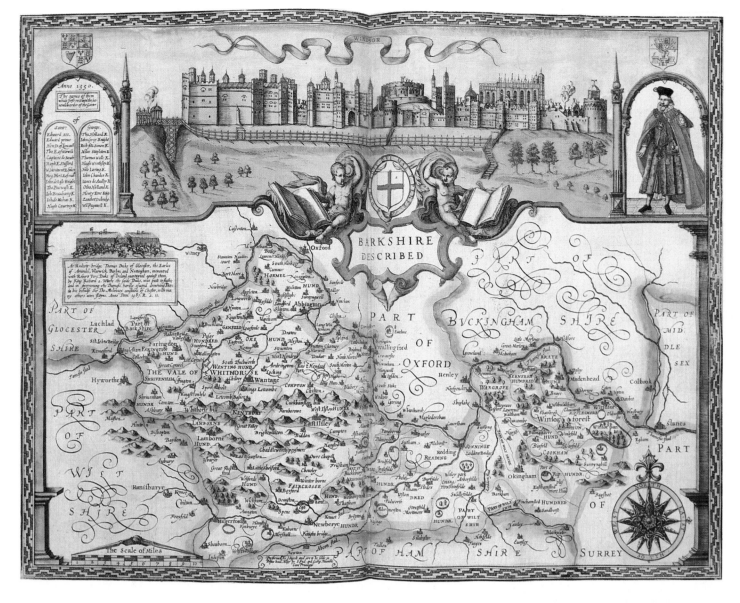

for nothing happened. Henceforth, it was downhill all the way —the Danes roamed at will, pillaging riverside settlements on the Thames as well as the coast. The prophecy was fulfilled in a sense, for once the Danes had set foot on Cwichelm's Law, they never again reached the coasts and left completely.

Ethelred's only solution was to marry the Norman Duke's daughter, Emma (or Aelfgifu to the Saxons), and to pay enormous sums in bribes to the invader. Neither saved his country, and the end soon came, when Cnut (Canute), the Danish leader, was chosen king by the Saxons after Ethelred's death. Cnut married Emma, and the result was twenty years' comparative peace for the country. Cnut was magnanimous to the conquered and tried to observe some of the local customs. He divided the kingdom, setting ealdormen over Mercia and Northumbria, but kept Wessex for himself, thus following Saxon tradition.

Cnut's death started a new wave of anarchy, when his sons, legitimate and bastard, contended for the throne. The English were relieved to welcome back the Saxon Edward, son of Ethelred and Emma, as true heir of the old line. This was where they were wrong, for he was weak and even more corrupt than his father. He started by taking all his mother's possessions and went on to grant ill-advised favours to Normans and Frenchmen who flocked to England with him. A tendency to dodge criticism by withdrawing into prayer and a religious trance has given him the soubriquet of 'Confessor' and an undeserved reputation for saintliness. As a king, he was a flop and he left England the prey of thugs. His successor, Harold, was at least an English thug, but was rapidly defeated by William of Normandy, known as The Conqueror.

Abingdon Rules O.K.?

During all the changes of kingship, one place which seems to have prospered was Abingdon Abbey. Berkshire was the centre of the country normally held by the Saxons, and it was in the Abingdon area where the royal wives and children lived for long periods. There was once a city and palace at a place called Seveocham or Schevechesam, which was destroyed in the worst time. Possibly it is represented by Shippon in Abingdon. When the place was re-established, it became known as Abingdon, which might be Afon-ton, the settlement by the river. The site is by a huge loop of the river Isis, at its junction with the river Ock.

There was a religious house at Sunningwell originally, removed for safety to the isle of Andersey, within the loop of the river, but when King Offa realised the defensive possibilities of Andersey, he exchanged it for a west bank site, to which the small abbey moved. Thereafter, monarch after monarch gave it grants of land and gifts of money. The precise dating of the grants is uncertain, because some Victorian worthies of Abingdon, finding the town rather full of grimy old bits of parchment none of them could read, threw most of them out. This act of vandalism wiped out Abingdon's early history.

The Abbots of Abingdon were 'mitred'—that is, they were on a level with Bishops, and took their place *ex officio* on the King's council. On occasion, an Abbot of Abingdon became Bishop of London or Archbishop of Canterbury—they often provided a safe home for the Archbishop or sundry bishops whose own sees were in a dangerous area. Edward the Confessor appointed his own cousin, Bishop Rudolf as Abbot in 1051.

The diplomatic skill of successive abbots can be inferred from the fact that they remained in favour, whoever was king. It was not so surprising that Cnut favoured them—he wanted to make friends with his people. What is startling is that after the Conquest, when the Normans generally had a massive clear-out and replaced all personnel with new men, William I not only continued the current abbot in office, but entrusted his youngest son, Henry, to the abbey to educate. Possibly there is some connection with the events of 1072, when the rebellious Bishop of Durham, Aethelwine, was defeated in battle and sent for safe-keeping by the king to Abingdon 'where he very soon passed away'.

Henry learned his lessons well. He may have been a compulsive womaniser, with 100 royal bastards acknowledged, he may have cheated his elder brother Robert out of the throne of England, and also the money compensation he was promised, but he was an excellent scholar—'Beauclerc' was his sobriquet—and his administrative system was strong and complex and in his time, the country was reasonably peaceful and began to weld into a whole. The Normans were on top, but there were not enough of them to control every detail of day-to-day living. Henry married Eadith, daughter of the King of Scotland, whose mother was the heiress of the old Saxon line, and a number of his barons also took English wives. More important, they entrusted their children to English nurses to bring up for their first vital six years. The power of the English nanny was clearly shown in a couple of generations by the stubborn identification of men like Richard de Clare and William de Montacute with England and the almost casual way in which the Anglo-Norman barons reacted to the loss of Normandy in John's reign.

Abingdon Abbey was incredibly rich. When all land ownership was listed in the Domesday Book in 1086, Abingdon had thirty-five manors in Berkshire and land in other counties, plus extensive 'baronial' powers over local justice and trading in and around the town. The power of the abbot was total and often abused, so that those who knew him best—the townsfolk of Abingdon—hated him as an oppressor. In 1327, the townsmen combined with the Mayor and townsmen of Oxford to attack and burn part of the Abbey and drive out the monks, but the well-connected Abbot came back with soldiers and hanged a dozen ringleaders. In 1431, the men of Abingdon rose again against their Abbot, swearing 'they would make the heads of the clergy as cheap as sheep's heads, 3 or 4 a penny'.

To counter the influence of the abbey, a Fraternity of the Holy Cross was founded by town merchants and they built an alternative church, St Helen's. This was originally quite small but later enlarged by side chapels, so that it is now broader than it is long. Public benefaction went to the Fraternity, not the Abbey, though the latter continued to live off its fat for long. Its power gradually declined until eventually it was seized and expropriated by Henry VIII at the Dissolution of the Monasteries. The townsfolk did nothing to defend their Abbey or Abbot who, true to form, cheerfully agreed to hand over the treasures and manors, provided he was given a fat pension and life tenancy of Cumnor Hall. Once he and the monks (who didn't fare so well) were out, the townsfolk started dismantling the place, using the stones for building houses and the lovely group of almshouses which surround the churchyard of St Helen's.

The only parts of the Abbey which survive, known as the Prior's House and the Guest House, were taken over and converted to a brewery, which gave a more agreeable reputation to the town than the greedy abbots had.

The other important feature of Abingdon was its bridge, built by Geoffrey Barbour and Sir Peter Bessils in 1416, which was a double structure, first crossing the Isis to Andersey Island at the Boroughford or Burford end, then proceeding by causeway across the island to Culham-ford, where the smaller stream was bridged and the road carried on to Dorchester, the Cathedral town, and linked with Wallingford, then the county town. However, this road and bridge combination not only ruined the trade for the Culham Ferry—which just happened to be owned by the abbey, and led to their hunting manor of Sutton Courtenay and the east; it also affected Wallingford, since, once the Thames/Isis had been crossed by westbound traffic from

Gloucester or Bristol to London, they did not want to re-cross to Wallingford town and pay new tolls, so tended to carry on down the Oxford bank to Henley, or cut across east to Watlington. Abingdon bridge was free of tolls, which made it worth a detour if you were a merchant carrying goods to London. Oxford also lost a certain amount of through trade, but Oxford could stand it.

Abingdon was an important clothing town in its day, and although the local merchants had to pay levies to the hated Abbey, they became very prosperous, which is why they were able to stand against the Abbey and pay for riots. As the wool trade declined, some of the expertise went into the weaving of sacks and canvas sails, but the old tradition died hard, and even at the beginning of this century, there was a busy little clothing factory which employed large numbers of out-workers in the villages around.

The breweries set up in the Abbey (which did continue a long tradition of monastic brewing) developed into a very important part of Abingdon trade, and two modern firms, Morlands and Ushens, still have their headquarters in the town.

The rise of Reading

Oddly enough, the man who reduced the prominence of Abingdon Abbey, was its own pupil, Henry I. Pure chance, or the workings of divine providence, which the oppressed townsfolk prayed for, directed his favours to Reading instead.

The town was reduced to a village of twenty-eight households in 1086, and although its useful position by the river enabled

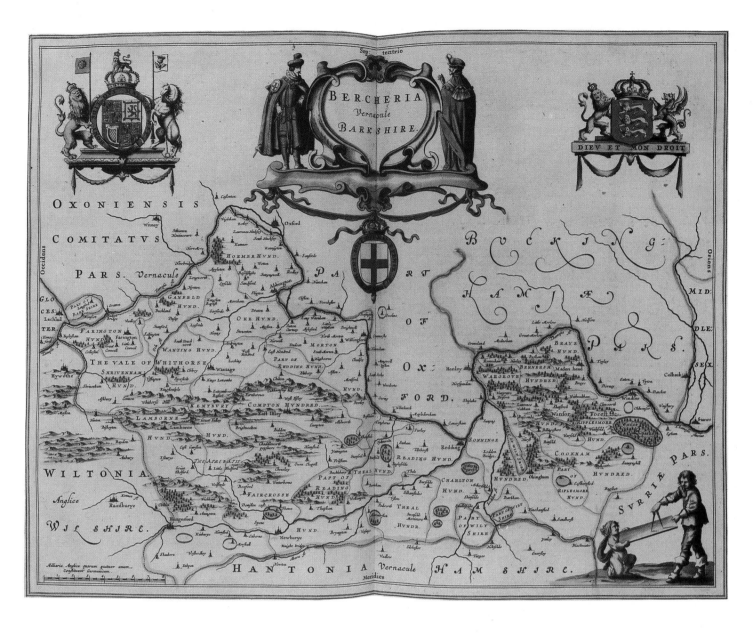

some recovery, it was luck that Henry happened to be there when the news came of the death of his only legitimate son, William, in the White Ship, in 1120. Sorrow led Henry to endow a great Abbey, at first built in wood, then stone. His frequent visits with his officials required a castle to be built too, for his defence. Parliaments and courts of justice, which followed the King, were often held here. Henry, his second wife and his daughter, as well as some royal bastards, were buried there. It was in this Abbey that the first pop song was written in about 1240. The catchy tune of 'Sumer is icumne in, lhude singe cucu' has ensured its durable appeal.

Henry II domolished the castle but continued to use the Abbey as a Parliament chamber occasionally. In 1183, the Patriarch of Jerusalem handed over the city keys here. It was part of the royal circuit roughly every three years until Edward II's time and on occasion after that. The town was fought over in the Civil War, but effectively, the royal connection ended here. However, the medieval status of the town ensured its emergence as County town later.

Reading's prosperity was founded on the wool trade. Relations between Abbey and town were not so acerbic as at Abingdon, but the trade guilds preserved their independence, building the magnificent church of St Lawrence in about 1400, next to their market place. After the Abbey, which had a second life as a minor palace, was pulled down, the stones were used for St Mary's, and there were also St Giles and Greyfriars parishes, which gives some idea of the size of the town.

Brewing was also important in Reading, and Simonds are still to the fore. Nowadays, the dominant industry is biscuit making,

at the long established Huntley and Palmer factory. Agricultural machinery is made and the extensive nursery of the horticultural seedsmen, Sutton's, adds a note of colour.

Royal Berks

There had been a Saxon palace of sorts at Windsor, but this was little more than a hunting lodge. William I gave it to the Archbishop of Canterbury, then had second thoughts, and took it back, because he had realised that this was at the north end of a magnificent tract of forest, stretching right across to Hampshire, which was full of huntable livestock. William 'loved the tall deer as he were their father'! Windsor was an ideal starting point, and he wisely raised a mound to fortify it, which became the base of the Round Tower later.

William Rufus kept occasional court here while he was hunting, which meant that extra buildings were erected piecemeal to house the court, and Henry I married Adeliza of Louvaine, his second wife, here in 1121. He had to marry because of the death of his heir, after which 'he never smiled again'. Another thing he didn't do was to father another heir, in fourteen years of marriage, though his tally of bastards before this was impressive. At fifty odd, he was worn out—it was not the lady's fault, since she was young and pretty, and when she remarried in 1135, after Henry's death, produced half a dozen children by her second husband, William d'Albini.

The only legitimate heir was Henry's daughter, Matilda. She was married young to old Emperor Henry and kept the title of Empress when she remarried the young puppy, Geoffrey of

Anjou. By him she had two sons, Henry and Geoffrey, and her father tried to ensure the succession to her and them. However, the barons did not fancy a female ruler, and settled for her cousin, Stephen of Blois, who was male and seemed an agreeable —and pliable—character. This was their mistake, since he set out to plunder the foreign country for himself and his cronies. For 'nineteen long winters' his men and the worst of the barons enjoyed themselves in uncontrolled extortion, robbery and savage torture.

The better sort of barons invited the Empress back, deciding she would have been a better Queen, or even King, than Stephen. She invaded and sporadic civil war ensued, when the only thing which saved Stephen was his own Queen, also Matilda, and a cousin on the mother's side of the Empress. At one stage, the Empress was captured, but escaped from Oxford across the frozen Thames in a white cloak to the haven of Wallingford Castle, always held for her by Brian Fitzcount, its lord, and soon after, a Treaty of Wallingford was signed, which allowed Stephen to rule for life, but gave the Empress's Henry the succession to England then, and Normandy at once.

Wallingford, the 'old fort at the ford' was important from Roman times and though the Saxon fort was burnt in 1006, it was rapidly rebuilt, and strengthened. At the Conquest it was owned by Wigo the Saxon, who came to terms with William and married off his heiress to a Norman, Robert d'Oyley. Robert built a castle, often used as a royal prison for dissidents. Robert's heiress married Brian Fitz-Count, the champion of Matilda the Empress. However, the line stopped here, for his sons caught leprosy and the sorrowing parents retired to religious houses.

Henry II took the honour (senior barony) of Wallingford into royal hands in 1154 and rewarded the town for supporting his mother's cause so loyally by unprecedented grants of trading privileges. 'His' merchants of Wallingford could trade anywhere in England, Normandy or Anjou without paying duties or taxes, and not subject to the normal judicial control of baronial courts. Anyone who demanded payment would be fined £10, a huge sum then. As far as I know, this grant has never been repealed and it is open to any Wallingford tradesman to test the point with the tax commissioners, or even the French courts.

Henry II gave Wallingford to his brother Richard Earl of Cornwall, who had been born there in 1209. It was a wedding present, and the honeymoon was spent there. Richard was immensely wealthy, since he was as extortionate as his brother, but a better business man. Henry gave away his ill gotten gains to his half-kin, the Lusignans, and his in-laws, the Provencals. These foreigners were so hated that the old Norman barons made common cause with the English against them. Richard's son, Edmund of Cornwall, named after St Edmund Rich, the Abingdon boy who became Archbishop of Canterbury, was approached to be champion of the 'English' (the Anglo-Norman barons) against the 'French', but wasn't up to it, or to producing an heir, so Wallingford went back to the Crown.

The next king, Edward II, gave it to his bon ami, Piers Gaveston, who also took the title of Earl of Cornwall. The barons were furious, since estate and title were royal—and kings ought to have mistresses. Gaveston was executed, but Edward found a new favourite, Hugh Despencer, who also held the manor and title until he too was executed, in 1326, by the hetero-sexual majority, headed by the slighted queen, Isabella, and her lover.

After this, Wallingford declined in importance, being used as a parking place for dowagers. Joan of Kent, widow of the Black Prince, was beauty enough in mature years to attract a retinue of hangers-on. Henry V's widow, Catherine of France, lived here in seclusion, comforted by the presence of her equerry, Sir Owen Tudor, who became her secret husband and father of Edmund Tudor, not necessarily in that order. Edmund married Margaret Beaufort, and their son, Henry Tudor, became by default the Lancastrian heir and king as Henry VII in 1485. Henry VIII gave Wallingford to Wolsey in his years of favour, but after that, it was a mere outpost, garrisoned for the King and loyal to Charles I, under its Captain, Thomas Blagge, during the Civil War. It was eventually captured and razed to the ground in 1646.

Back to Windsor

Henry III started to improve Windsor and built the Round Tower, plus a great hall, kitchen and chapel, of which only the former remains. Edward III, who happened to be born there, selected the architect cum clerk of works who created the Castle as we know it. This was his chaplain, William of Wykeham, later Bishop of Winchester, who did a better job than most professionals, and went on to build Winchester College and New College. For Windsor, he was paid a basic shilling a day and the chief mason, William Winford, probably got less.

All counties were obliged to contribute masons, tilers and carpenters, and when the first lot were devastated by plague, the King sent for more, until there were too few men left to get in the harvest. Glaziers were called for in 1363 and the main work was complete by 1369. It comprised the Great Quadrangle, the 'Palace' or living quarters, St George's Hall, the first St George's chapel, domestic offices and housing for the clergy and military knights of Windsor.

The castle became now more of a fortress than a hunting lodge, and was used to house important prisoners, like David, King of Scotland and John of France, who both suggested refinements. James I of Scotland as a prince was imprisoned there, and fell in love with Lady Jane Beaufort, one of the Queen's ladies, who became his bride.

The larger and more comfortable Windsor became, the less use was made of Reading Abbey. In any case, administrative functions were being concentrated more at Westminster or the Tower, so the Berkshire connection became less official and more ceremonial and domestic.

Whose Garter?

The traditional story of the founding of the Order of the Garter is that 'Joan, Countess of Salisbury' dropped her blue garter at a Court ball. Edward III retrieved it, placed it on his leg, remarked *'Honi soit qui mal y pense'* (Evil be to him who thinks evil). Edward founded the Order of the Garter, with that motto and the blue ribbon badge, in 1346. The Garter is the personal gift of the sovereign and numbers are limited to twenty-six, of whom the Prince of Wales is always one.

The Earls of Salisbury were the Montacutes, then of Bisham.

Donnington Park Estate
by Jonathan Godfrey, 1654

In contrast to general county maps, estate surveys allow a microscopically detailed view of the landscape and give unique information for the local historian. They are often works of art in their own right. Jonathan Godfrey, the surveyor of this fine map of Donnington Park Estate, justifiably styled himself "artist".

Godfrey records the extent and arrangement of Robert Packer's estate in 1654. The Packer family arms are shown at the top right. In the sixteenth century the park was recorded as a preserve of deer and game so the small figures with guns on "The Mountain" may well be a hunting party. The tower surrounded by rabbits indicates the fourteenth century gatehouse of Donnington Castle. In the fifteenth century it was owned by Thomas Chaucer, probably the son of the poet, but its chief moment of glory was during the Civil War. It was then owned by John Packer, secretary to the Duke of Buckingham. When he and his son, Robert, refused funds to Charles I and joined the Parliamentarian side, their land was sequestered by the King, and John Boys held the Castle.

John Packer died in 1649—the same year as Charles I. His son regained his estates and was MP for Wallingford both during the Commonwealth and the reign of Charles II. The estate map might almost be a celebration of property restored. The castle was badly damaged during the Civil War and only the gatehouse stands today although some of the outer defences dug by Sir John Boys's men can still be traced on the ground. (By kind permission of D.A. Hartley Russell Esq.)

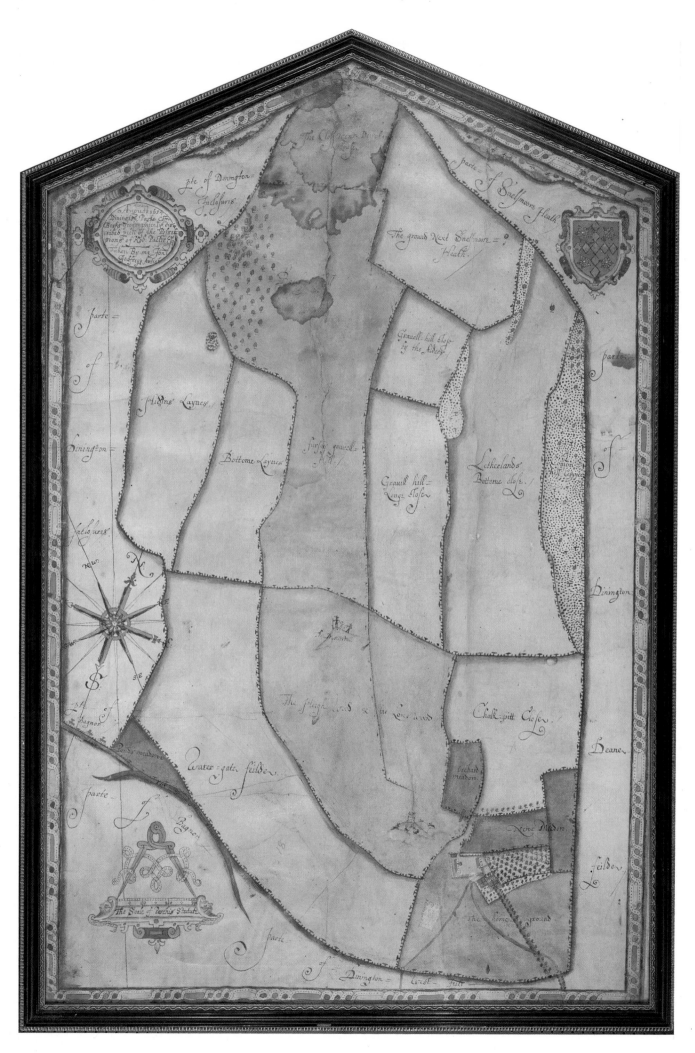

Edward III gave it to his supporter, William de Montacute, for his help in securing the throne, and William built an Augustinian Priory, with a fine reputation for hospitality. Many of his family are buried there. His young son, also William, inherited the title in 1343 and was betrothed, but not married, to Joan, 'the Fair Maid of Kent', granddaughter of Edward I, already a promising beauty of fourteen. The slightly older William went off to the French Wars, coming back in 1346 to claim his bride.

But Joan, startlingly, preferred Thomas Holland, son of a knight, who had been her father's squire. He was fourteen years older, one-eyed and battle scarred, and all he had to recommend him was a fund of war hero stories and a modest fortune from ransoming French prisoners. Joan claimed they had been betrothed when she was a child, tumbled into bed and told the world about it. Young Salisbury gave her up, and she married Sir Thomas in 1348. He became Earl of Kent in her right in 1360.

In 1346, the actual Countess of Salisbury was William's widowed mother, Catherine de Grandison, fortyish and no great beauty. Joan was a dazzler and her code of morals elastic. It has been suggested that the blue garter was the badge of a witch coven, to which the King belonged as well. Dropping a garter was commonplace. Dropping a witchcraft sign was dangerous, and the enigmatic motto therefore makes sense.

After Thomas's death, Joan married the Prince of Wales (the Black Prince) in 1361. For a widow of thirty-two, with a dubious past, to marry the heir to the throne is surprising, but possibly the King felt that his son, unmarried at thirty one, would never continue the succession. The Prince died before his father, and Joan spent her widowhood at Wallingford, where a stream of

Berkshire by Robert Morden, 1695

In 1695, Edmund Gibson, Fellow of Queen's College, Oxford, and future Bishop of London, published a new edition of William Camden's Britannia. *Camden's history had first appeared over a century earlier in 1586, and Gibson felt it could be improved. He included a series of maps intended to be from "the newest Surveys that have been made, together with all the Roads exactly mapped out". Before this scheme few county maps had shown roads. John Norden had occasionally included them and, in 1675, John Ogilby had published his strip-road itinerary, also entitled* Britannia. *In the following year a London bookseller, Robert Morden (fl.1669–1703) produced a set of playing cards decorated with county maps, the first series to show main roads. He specialised in geographical subjects, working from his aptly named shop* The Atlas, *firstly in Cheapside and later Cornhill. Edmund Gibson gave him the commission for his new* Britannia *maps.*

Morden had to select the best maps available—including Ogilby's Britannia—*but these were often based on Elizabethan surveys. He updated them from local information, sending copies to advisers for correction, and so created the "new survey". Edmund Gibson was unhappy with the work and his doubts were justified for it was strongly criticized as inaccurate when it was published.*

In spite of these attacks, Morden's series is an advance in county mapping. His "Berkshire" is unfussy, allowing the roads to show clearly. For the first time the major routes through the county, especially the important Bath and Bristol road, are defined. Evidence of some local information appears in the town plans, more modern spellings, churches and landmarks such as Donnington Castle and a few mills. Degrees from St Paul's Cathedral are at the bottom of the map and minutes along the top (this was the first time that the differences of local time were indicated on a set of county maps). Because of inconsistencies in the lengths of local and statute miles, there are three scales.

Criticism of Morden seems unfair. He was never offered the finance or opportunity to undertake a proper survey and Gibson's extravagant claims for "the newest Surveys" must have raised expectations. The maps were, after all, intended only to complement a history "carrying the eye of the Reader from place to place as he peruses the text". (By courtesy of Robert Douwma Prints and Maps Ltd)

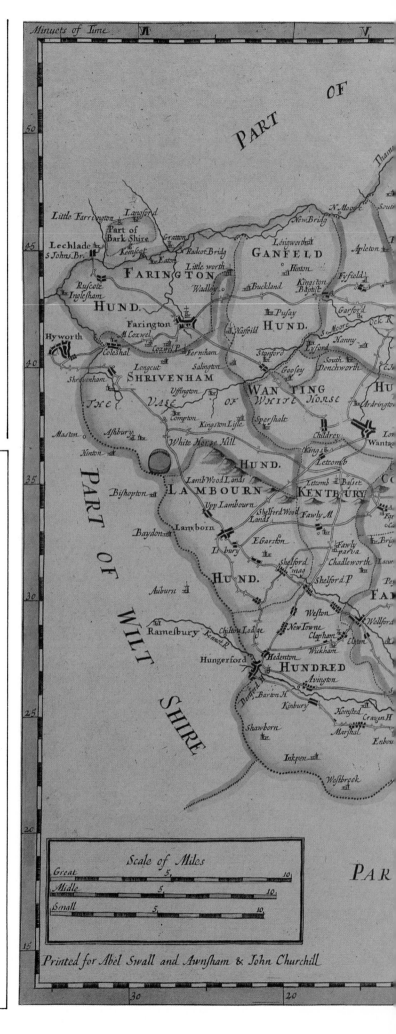

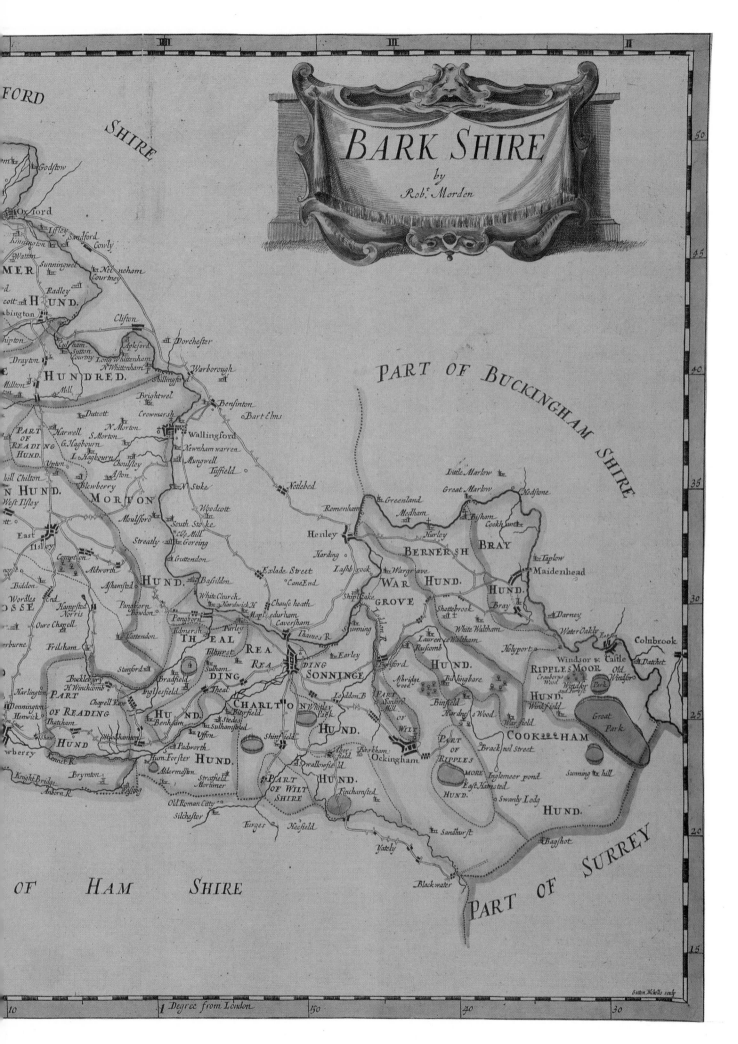

BARK SHIRE
by
Rob. Morden

xiii

courtiers sought her out to use her influence with her son, Richard II.

St George's chapel, a cathedral in size and status, is the home of the Garter Knights, and the Military Knights of Windsor, originally pensioners of the king. From Edward IV's time, many royal baptisms and marriages have occurred there, and burials in the royal Mausoleum at Frogmore nearby.

King and Super King

Also associated with Bisham was a man who, in his time, was more powerful than the King. In fact, he decided who was to be King. The Montacute heiress married Richard Neville, in her right, Earl of Salisbury, and their son, Richard also, married the heiress of Warwick, so he is known to history as Richard, Earl of Warwick, or the 'Kingmaker'.

In turn, he put the Yorkist Edward IV and the Lancastrian Henry VI on the throne, and was heaped with titles and rewards by both, so that he was worth the immense sum of 80,000 crowns apart from his inheritance. His two daughters married into both royal branches and one had surviving children who were dangerous to the Crown. Warwick himself was killed in battle, and is buried at Bisham, beside his parents, and his grandson, Edward of Clarence, kept a prisoner by Henry VII until his mysterious death. The last descendant, Margaret, Countess of Salisbury, was suddenly deemed a menace, at the age of seventy-two, and beheaded. Henry VIII took Bisham and gave it to his divorced wife, Anne of Cleves, the 'Flanders Mare'. She exchanged it with the Hobys for a manor in Kent, and that was the end of the Royal connection.

Berkshire by John Rocque, 1752–61

A large section of Berkshire's history and tradition has now been lost to Oxfordshire through the boundary changes of 1974. A detail from "A Topographical Map of the County of Berks, by John Rocque" (1752–61) shows the northern border of the county running west along the banks of the Thames to beyond Lechlade.

John Rocque's map was the first large-scale map of Berkshire—on a scale of two inches to the mile. It was published on eighteen sheets which could be joined for display as a wall-map or bound into a book, so it was intended for a wealthy clientele with libraries, large houses, and, above all, the money to subscribe to Rocque's work.

The startling change in mapping, made possible by the change of scale, is obvious, for details down to individual houses, barns, mills and bridleways are marked. Rocque, a Huguenot from Geneva, also introduced continental techniques to show different types of land. Without needing a key, rough pasture, woods, hills and farmland were engraved in ways that could be understsood easily. Gone were the vague molehills for downland and single trees for woods found on earlier maps. The mapsheets were published in stages and subscribers were invited to make corrections "with thanks, and no Additional Expence". In spite of this, the map is not as accurate in detail as it might seem. The scale of the fields is not in proportion and industry was often ignored, but the general impression does give a true and fascinating picture of mid-eighteenth century Berkshire just before land enclosures and the growth of cereal farming were to change the landscape drastically.

John Rocque (c.1703–62) began his career drawing plans of gardens and houses of the nobility, including the Royal gardens at Richmond and Windsor. George II admired Rocque's plan of Dublin so much that it was hung in his own apartment, and, by the time the Berkshire map was published, Rocque could state proudly on the title that he was "Topographer to His Majesty". With a life full of commissions, support from Royalty and a reputation for the high quality of his work, Rocque would appear to have been a successful man. However, he died poor. The struggle to finance his mapping projects—as in so many other cases—left little margin for profit. (By courtesy of the British Library)

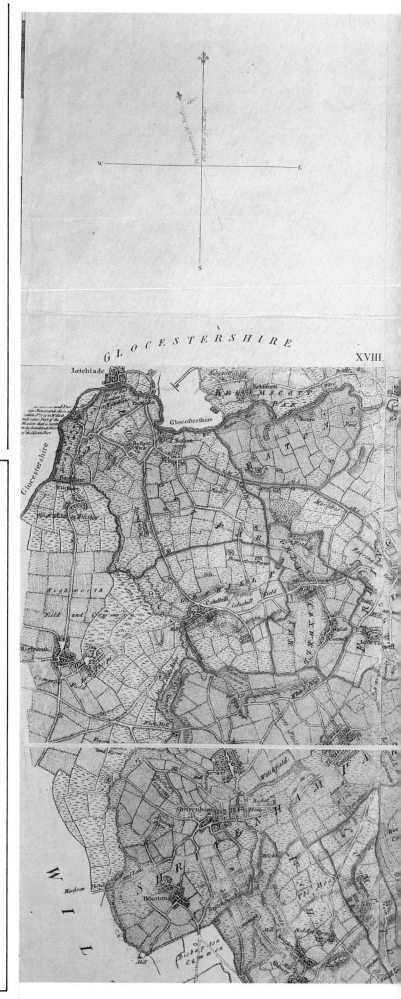

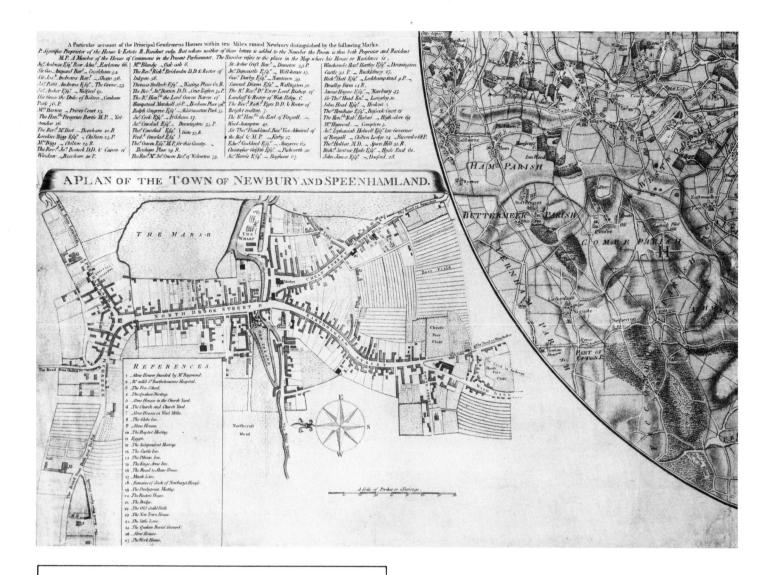

Down in the forest

Most of Berkshire was still covered by forest which was the way the kings liked it since their interest was in hunting, not agriculture. The king held so much of the county in royal demesne (or personal control) that it tended to stay that way, at least in the south. However, Abingdon Abbey owned thirty-five manors, and Reading Abbey was also well endowed out of the royal lands. Rapidly, the Abbot there came into collision with his tenants at Blewbury for increasing rents and imposing taxes, and they appealed, as old royal tenants. The medieval equivalent of the rent tribunal, which included a 'serjeant-keeper' for every village in Berks and eighteen free men from Blewbury, fixed the amount due at just less than halfway between what the tenants wanted to pay and what the Abbot demanded.

Other manors were given to body servants of the king—the man who looked after the royal pipes of wine was given Creswell in Bray, and the man who bought the beer got West Hendred. Henry de Ferrers, one of the clerks who collected the information for the Domesday Book, was given huge grants of land, mainly in the north midlands, from which his son drew his title of Earl of Derby, but also odd manors scattered about the country, including Berkshire. At first, his tenants had to travel north to the baronial court at Tutbury, Staffs, but later he granted his outlying manors to his own knights, including Hubert de Curzun, who got Lockinge. The Berkshire line died out, but the junior line were the Curzons of Kedleston, Earl Howe and Viscount Scarsdale.

In most villages, the villeins and free tenants were quietly increasing their potential acreage by clearing the forest back a little. The local lords were happy about this since it increased their own manor and rentals but if the king, as lord of all the land, and friend of the stag, found out, there was trouble. Making 'assarts' or clearings, defined as any place where a man standing on a stump of a tree could see five other stumps round him, drew fines at least. Richard I sent stump-hoppers round Berkshire, and fined the villages of Bucklebury, Kentwood, Beech Hill, Grazeley, Whitley, Thatcham, Sonning and Earley half a mark each. This was a lot of money, and even the clerks in the office thought that the foresters (under Alan de Neville, chief forester and his kin) were greedy. It may have been a Berkshire man who scribbled 'Richard de Neville is black and a bad man' on the accounts.

Even the villages profited from the existence of the great wool towns since there was a ready market for their sheep and other produce. Technically, serfs belonged to the lord of the Manor, but if they could get to a chartered town and live for a year and a day, they were free. The existence of chartered towns with a high demand for workers kept the lords of the manor in order, since if they were cruel, all the serfs would run away. Berkshire lords got into a habit of quiet and peaceable living, which, with very few exceptions, characterised the county gentry from then on.

A wealth of wool

The weaving of wool cloth for more than domestic requirements was encouraged by the Norman kings, who imported Flemish weavers and processors to improve English cloth. Edward III offered positive patronage by wearing English woven garments only, and his support enabled English cloth merchants to dominate the market, supplying wool to the Flemings and cloth to the (then) world.

Berkshire was in the forefront of this boom. Thomas Cole of Reading was reputed to be the agent who pulled off the Flemish deal and the towns of Reading, Abingdon and Newbury, and the village of Hendred in particular 'stood by cloth', with Cloth Fairs and Cloth Halls controlled by gilds of merchants, though the great abbeys competed for a share. There were huge flocks of sheep on the Downs to supply raw material and a general air of prosperity reigned until export restrictions were imposed during the Wars of the Roses for political reasons.

The status quo was restored largely through the efforts of John Winchcombe (or Smalwode), the archtypal successful clothier, whose fictionalised autobiography, *The Adventures of Jacke of Newbury*, was written in 1597 by Thomas Deloney, himself a silk weaver, who also wrote the less successful *Thomas (Cole) of Reading*.

It tells of the diligent apprentice who married his widowed mistress and her business and after her death chose a blonde servant maid as his second lady. Jack had two hundred looms, each attended by a man and a quill-making boy; a hundred female carders, two hundred female spinners; ninety poor children employed as sorters; fifty shearman; eight 'towers' (rovers); forty dyers and twenty fullers. All these were fed on the premises and it took ten fat steers a week to provide the meat, which meant a full-time butcher, baker and brewer, five cooks and numerous scullions and maids. The various kerseys and broadcloths were stored in warehouses, employing yet more men.

Jack was a major employer and wealth producer. He was therefore assessed to send four pikemen and two horsemen to defend England from the Scots, as much as the local gentry who by custom provided 'knight service'. He was rich and loyal enough to send fifty horsemen and fifty pike and bowmen, magnificently dressed by the firm, to the rage of the gentry, whose contributions were little and late. Jack entertained Henry VIII and Katherine of Aragon and was offered a knighthood but bargained for the more useful lifting of trading restrictions with the Continent.

John Winchcombe did represent the shire in Parliament (usually a knight's job) and his son, John, was given the manor of Bucklebury at the Dissolution of the Monasteries. His son became a baronet as Sir Henry Winchcombe.

The fictionalised account may include conversations between the king and his wealthy subject which never happened but his importance, and the influence of clothiers in general, is indisputable. Many of them lent money to the king or nobles and were knighted themselves. The sixteenth century was their highpoint when everyone wore wool for normal dress and the powerful gilds of merchants took over the town administration from the crumbling abbeys. International contacts probably did produce the gift of 'ten tunnes of Rhenish wine' for John's second wedding and there was constant movement of Berks clothiers' sons to London and Europe, which promoted the flow of ideas as well as money.

When changing fashions and renewed war reduced the sales of English wool cloth, the government, tender of this important trade, decreed in 1666 and again in 1678 that no corpse should be buried unless it was 'wrapp'd in sheep's wool only'. And to enforce the law, the nearest and dearest should make an affidavit before a magistrate to that effect. These registers of 'Buryalls in Woollen' are still found among parish records today, although in most places the enforcement lapsed before the law was repealed in 1813. Oddly enough, it became the rule for the rich, including families of magistrates, to break the law, since being buried in silk or linen was punished by a forced donation to the parish Poor Box, and the locals thought it meant to cheat them out of the money.

The cartouches on Emanuel Bowen's county maps are often highly informative about the particular region. Many aspects of Berkshire life are represented on this late edition of Bowen's "An Accurate Map of Berkshire divided into hundreds" (1775?). Woollen cloth, the foremost industry of earlier centuries, is shown with a sheaf of barley to indicate the malting industry. The famous trout of the River Kennet are there, while an incongruous pile of regalia symbolises the Royal connection with the county. In the background, a Thames barge carries goods upriver. (By courtesy of the British Library)

Even so, the wool trade declined steadily in the south. It was accelerated in East Hendred, because James I took against the squire and people and set up a rival cloth market at East Ilsley. Hendred folk sensibly transferred their skills to the weaving and sale of linen. With the coming of steam, the vast majority of woollen manufacture moved to the mills of Yorkshire where there was coal to hand—just in time for the broadcloth boom of Victorian times.

However, Berks went down fighting. In 1811 in Buckland, a sheep was sheared at 5am, the wool cleaned, carded and spun, the cloth woven, dyed and cut into a suit, which the local lord of the manor, Sir John Throckmorton, wore at a trade dinner in Newbury that night. The time taken, from the sheep's back to Sir John's, was 13 hours 20 minutes.

East Ilsley, James's favourite, lost its weavers with the rest in the county, when hand looms went out of fashion, but it retained the great Sheep Fair until this century. There were permanent sheep pens in the main street and up to 80,000 sheep could pass through in a day. Mutton was more popular with Victorian families than it is now, being the staple diet for children and the moderately poor. Several other towns thronged with sheep on market day too, and several writers report being unable to distinguish animals from farmers.

Most of the weaving towns went over to manufacturing sacking, sail-canvas and any sort of coarse fabric. In Wokingham, there was a silk-weaving factory from early times but this foundered when French silk was allowed in without tariffs.

The New Men

The Wars of the Roses exhausted the old baronial class and left the way clear for the 'novi homines' (new men), who came in with the upstart Henry VII, whose claim to the throne was by conquest rather than pedigree. The new men bought up the old manors, some with fortunes made from wool or money-lending. To feel at home among the ranks of the gentry, they faked pedigrees connecting themselves with old baronial families and adopted fancy coats of arms, which their ancestors might have borne, had they not had the sense to stay out of battles and get rich at home.

Most of the Berkshire new men settled for the solidity of riches and wide lands. The best chance for pickings came at the Dissolution of the great abbeys of Reading and Abingdon and lesser priories round the county. Typical of the vultures were the Wellesbournes, Oliver and John, descended from a Bucks yeoman family who claimed Simon de Montfort as an ancestor, not realising that the Montforts of Wellesbourne were a different family.

They had the enviable task of distributing the goodies when Abingdon Abbey was dissolved, which they did to perfection, coming down hard on those who argued, giving small land or trading concessions to those who co-operated. The town hated the Abbey, the local gentry got their share, the King his larger one and the Abbot gladly took a bribe to go quietly, so the whole thing was managed without the noise raised at Reading, where the Abbot was hanged before his gates.

Oliver settled at West Hanney, probably in the 'Prior's House' by the church. His intention was to found a dynasty of knights or better, but his legitimate son was weakly and the male line ended there. The manor went to the Ayschcombes, who rose in the world, but gambled it all away in three generations. All that is left of the Wellesbourne ambition is some fine brasses before the altar.

Many Berkshire families were like this—the Hydes of Denchworth, the Yates of Lyford and Buckland, the Lattons of Kingston Bagpuize, the Aldworths of Wantage and so on. Some became knights, but they never reached the peerage. They stayed quietly on their manors, marrying the heiresses of neighbours, so they had a choice of houses within a limited area. They married into old knightly families like the Fettiplaces and Englefields, or merchanting ones like the Winchcombes, Spicers, Justices or Martins. They lived like comfortable farmers, with only the occasional show of silk and swords, if the King or some great magnate passed by.

Inevitably, sons of younger sons went into merchanting, or craft trades. Some prospered and bought more land but others, inevitably, struggled and failed, sinking into the general ranks of labourers. Most old Berks families can claim links with all social classes except possibly the highest.

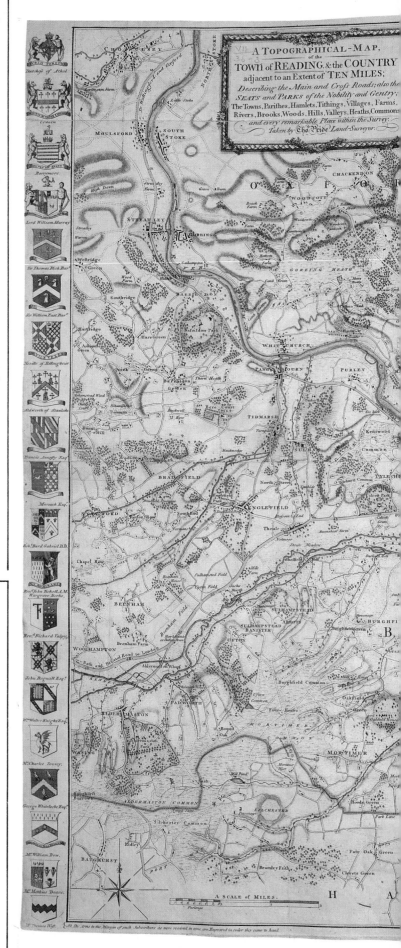

Reading and the Country Adjacent
by Thomas Pride and Philip Luckombe, 1790

Thomas Pride and Philip Luckombe's map of the environs of Reading (1790) may have been inspired by John Willis' similar map of the Newbury area in 1768. There was strong commercial rivalry between the two towns, which came to a head early in the century when navigation up the River Kennet to Newbury was improved. The inhabitants of Reading feared they might lose their monopoly as a trade centre, advantageously placed at the fork of the Kennet and Thames.

The scale of one-and-a-half-inches to the mile allows a wealth of detail on the map. The many turnpikes reflect the number of Turnpike Trusts set up in the eighteenth century in an attempt to improve stretches of roads. Unlike John Rocque's map of 1752–61, types of farmland are not specified, although open pasture is indicated. The eye-catching features of the map are the estates, drawn with enough precision to show the effects of fashionable landscaping.

Thomas Pride (fl.1758–97) was an estate surveyor based in Bloomsbury, London, so the emphasis on estates may derive from this experience. More importantly, the map was a commercial venture. It would have been vital for Pride to depict the estates with care as the estate owners—he hoped—would be buying the map. Around the edge are the coats-of-arms "of such subscribers as were received in time" and the map is dedicated to William Lord Craven, Lord Lieutenant of the County. (By courtesy of the British Library)

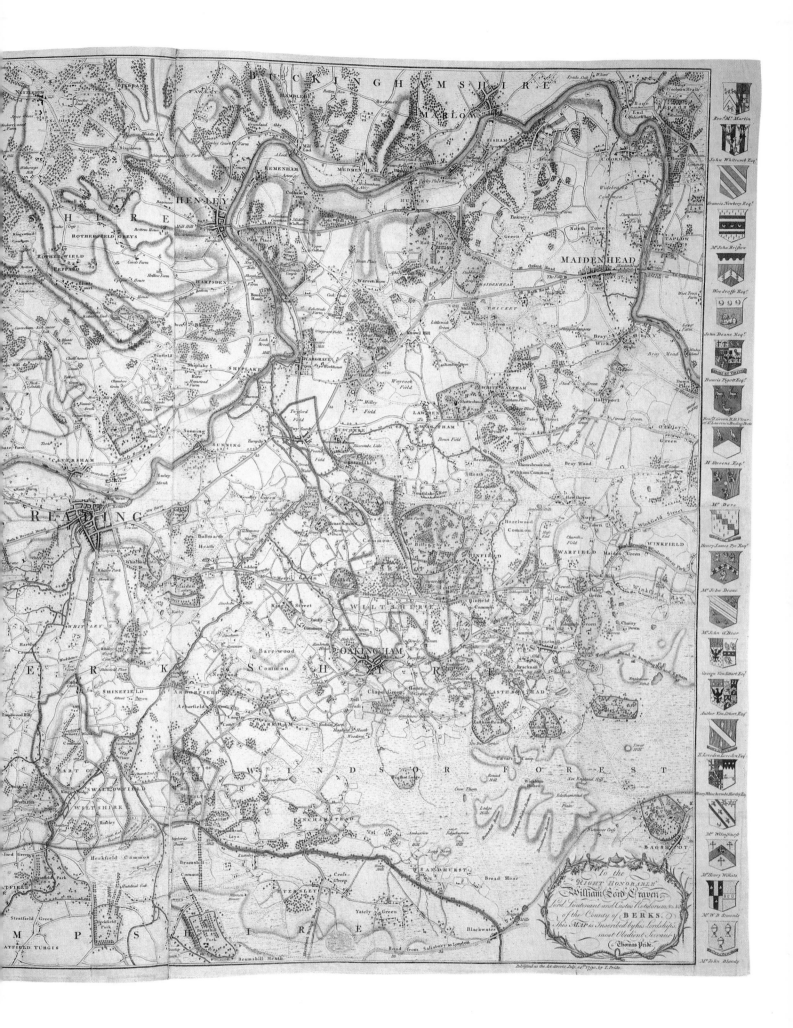

Blotted Copybook

A mysterious death is associated with Bisham Abbey, acquired by the Hoby family in the 1530s. Sir Thomas, diplomat, soldier, talented author and sometime guardian of the young Elizabeth, inherited in 1558. His young wife, Elizabeth, was one of the four clever daughters of Sir Anthony Cooke, tutor to Edward VI. He had them educated to a very high standard, as did a few of the best Elizabethan parents, so that they would be fitting mates for brilliant men. One married Lord Burleigh and was the mother of Robert Cecil, Earl of Salisbury; another married Sir Nicholas Bacon and was the mother of Francis, Lord Verulam, author and Attorney General.

Elizabeth Hoby had one quite bright son, Sir Edward, and another, Thomas Posthumous, who was undersized, conceited and venomous but a thorough dandy. Tradition says there was another son, William, who was so stupid he could not write without blotting his copybook. Elizabeth was said to be so furious she killed him. Education was an important matter and could be beaten into children, as it was in schools for many years to come.

No fuss was made at the time—children came and went with great speed and the loss of one dunce was hardly worth comment. What has preserved this story is that Lady Hoby was said to walk, wringing her hands in repentance. This I doubt: righteous indignation, anger, irritation, perhaps. Repentance, no. And there is no William in her family to be found. Yet his schoolbook with blotted pages was found, long after, signed William Hoby. I think that the child may have been her grandson, only legitimate child of Sir Edward. When he died, the estate went to Peregrine Hoby, his bastard by a mistress, Katherine Pinkeney. If Elizabeth killed the heir and let the child of the hated mistress take all, then she would have every reason to walk, from pure spite.

The Recusants

One reason why the gentry families of Berkshire lived rather retiring lives, instead of making an impact on the world, was that many of them were Catholics, at a time when that religion was forbidden and even feared. When Henry VIII broke with Rome, he expected all his subjects to follow him and, apart from the brief respite in Mary I's reign, the law enforced attendance at the parish church, with heavy fines for those who stayed away. These applied to Puritans too, but the real persecution was aimed at the old Catholic families. They were usually richer, more influential and had overseas connections which must be treasonable.

The Eystons claim proudly a relationship to Sir Thomas More, whose adherence to the faith caused his execution. They came to Berks in about 1450, when John Eyston married Isabel Stowe, heiress of line to the old Turberville and d'Arches lords of the manor of East Hendred. They married into local gentry families, not all openly Catholic at first, but later spouses were all impeccably 'Roman'. They built a chapel in their manor house for their own worship and had others at their Drayton house, and in the hidden hamlet of Catmore, where they could retire in difficult times. William Eyston was heavily fined for religion in Charles I's time, but remained loyal to the king, thus attracting reprisals from Cromwell's men on both counts.

It was often necessary to fake pedigrees and switch property from father to son, to avoid total loss, in Stuart times, and even in the 'Age of Enlightenment' of the eighteenth century, it paid to keep quiet if you were a Catholic. It was not until 1830 that Emancipation brought licence to worship as they pleased and to hold official positions in the community. Until 1830, no Eyston was a magistrate, member of Parliament, or even a customs officer. In 1831, Charles Eyston was appointed High Sheriff, the most senior honorary post in the county. His grandfather, Thomas John, a celebrated antiquary, collected a museum of relics of More, Archbishop Fisher and other Catholic martyrs, including Hugh Faringdon, Abbot of Reading, who refused to co-operate with Henry VIII's commissioners at the Dissolution, and was hanged at his own gates for it.

Sir Francis Englefield of Englefield (1520–96) was also a recalcitrant Catholic, but was appointed Sheriff of Berks before the sacrament test was introduced. He was committed to the Tower for allowing mass to be said in the household of Princess Mary Tudor, in 1551, but when she came to the throne was an M.P. and Privy Councillor. On Elizabeth's accession, he devised his property to a nephew and escaped to Spain, where he was involved in intrigues to promote the cause of Mary, Queen of Scots.

His estates were seized but later came into the hands of John Paulet, Marquess of Winchester, whose family were also Catholic, but more devious. His ancestor, Sir William Paulet, enjoyed the confidence of Henry VIII, and was Treasurer through the reigns of Edward VI, Mary and Elizabeth, despite the religious changes. Asked how he did it, he replied 'By being a willow, not an oak'. John was an 'oak', but for his staunch loyalty to Charles I was imprisoned in the Tower.

The Yates at Lyford also had their own chapel, and gave shelter to the famous priest, Edmund Campion in 1581. The Jesuit had a price on his head, and was captured on leaving the manor, and taken to London, where he was tortured and then hanged.

The Yates at Buckland were followed by the Throckmortons, and they too preserved relics of the martyrs, including Mary, Queen of Scots' chemise and a medal commemorating Charles I. The Fettiplaces had several manors around England but here are associated with Appleton, Childrey and Shefford.

The Barretts of Milton, near Abingdon, were a very private family, but one of the daughters married an Archer-Shee, a family whose scion became notorious as the original of *The Winslow Boy*.

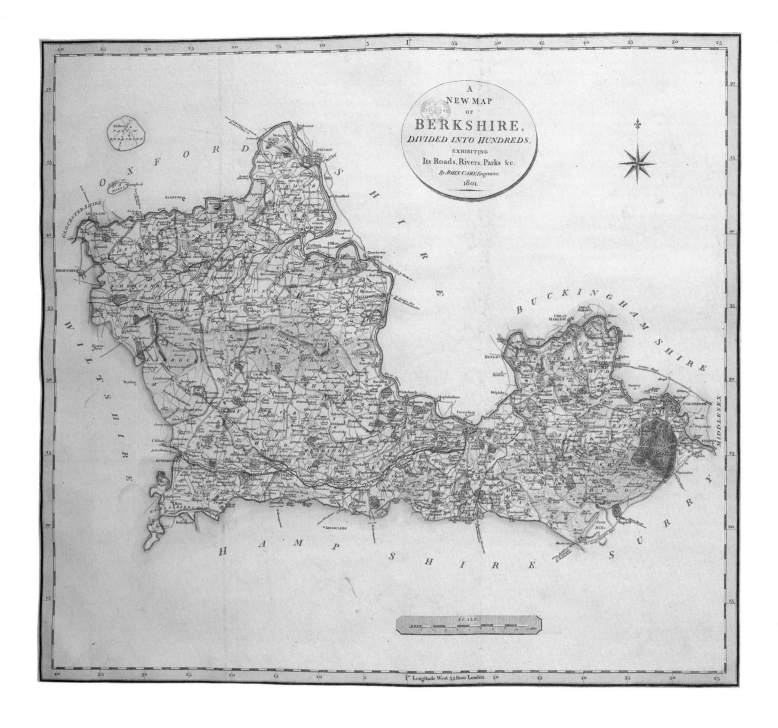

There were martyrs on the Protestant side too. In Newbury, Christian Shoemaker was burned for reading the gospels to his friends and Jocelyn Palmer, the master of Reading School, was burnt with two others in the 1540s. Many conversions to Catholicism in the last century were influenced by Edward Bouverie-Pusey, author of *Tracts for the Times*, and part of the 'Oxford Movement'. He himself never 'went over to Rome', but many other members did. In Tudor times, he would have been burned—in Victorian days, he was lionised by Society.

There were many Catholics in Berkshire, for each gentry family encouraged their tenants to use their private chapels and follow the faith. It is not surprising to find a Catholic school here. When it was difficult for Catholics to be educated in England, some English Benedictines founded a school at Douai, in France. They were expelled from France in 1904 and eventually settled the school at Woolhampton, where there had been a Catholic church since soon after emancipation.

King or Parliament?

Berkshire had the Civil War thrust upon it when Charles I, having lost his grip on London in the early days, chose Oxford as his new 'capital'. All roads to the important south and west ran through Berkshire, and because Bucks was fairly solidly pro-Parliament, so did the way to London and ultimate victory. The roads ran through Abingdon and Wallingford, along the Thames to Reading, for London; south through Abingdon and Newbury for Basing and the Hampshire coast; south west through Wantage and Hungerford towards Salisbury and Exeter; west through Abingdon, Wantage and Faringdon to Bristol, or, turning north from Faringdon to Cirencester, towards the loyal north-west.

In 1642 Governor Martin held Reading for Parliament but when the Royal army advanced triumphantly towards London, he moved out without firing a shot. When Charles was blocked at Brentford, he retired to Reading, but found the town 'very mean to endure a formed siege', so left Sir Arthur Aston in charge and went to Oxford. (Windsor, despite having a castle, was never taken seriously as a fortress.) Aston was desperately short of gunpowder (so was Charles) and when Parliament moved south and took Winchester, which endangered the route from the sea, and then Portsmouth and Chichester, the likeliest ports, it was impossible to hold Reading, and Essex took it. The Royal forces consolidated and advanced on Gloucester, where

Essex followed. He then realised he was cut off from base by a solid wodge of loyal Berks, with garrisons at Faringdon, Wantage, Wallingford and near Newbury. He shot back south of the county but was forced on to the main west road at Hungerford. The first battle of Newbury ensued, when only the London Trained Bands saved Essex from defeat. He burst through but lost many valuable officers, including Lord Sutherland, and the incomparable Lord Falkland was killed on the King's side. He was a man of great integrity, disliking much of Charles's policy and more of his followers, but faultlessly loyal to his anointed King.

The ascendancy of the King did not last long, but still this centre core of Berkshire was his. Abingdon was rather important, as it was on the best road to almost anywhere, and the Royal horses were usually kept there when not in use. In May, 1644, Wilmot, the governor of Abingdon, panicked when he heard that Essex was advancing again, and surrendered the town without firing a shot, though it was a splendid defensive position. From then, Major General Brown sat in Abingdon for the Parliament, even when the fiery Prince Rupert tried to dislodge him. The only Thames bridge for miles was lost, and all movements south had to be made via Wallingford from then on. Moreover, Brown 'infested Oxford much' since it could never be left lightly defended, with the enemy six miles away'.

The south of the county was held by the loyal John Boys at Donnington Castle, just north of Newbury town. High on the hill, the castle commanded the two roads, east–west and north–south, protected to the south by a loop of the river Lambourne. Boys (knighted in 1644) happily defended the battered castle against all comers, even when Colonel Middleton blasted down the corner towers with 'one thousand shot a day'. Now the sturdy gatehouse towers with the bases of the walls are all that remain, but from the castle hill, one can look round over the countryside, and realise what a very good strategic position it was. The enemy would have been visible for three miles at least and the artillery Charles entrusted to Boys could have been manoeuvred to face the attack.

The second battle of Newbury was fought at Donnington and round the fortified walls of Shaw House and other cosy manors in the vicinity, but Charles was put to flight, and could then have been totally crushed, but for gallant Donnington. Charles managed to relieve it again, and it continued to be almost as much a nuisance to the Parliamentary troops as their man in Abingdon was to Charles. However, small victories in Berks did not make up for general defeats elsewhere, and the war stuttered to a close.

Apart from Donnington, Wallingford had been consistently held for the King by Thomas Blagge, and its bridge was valuable after Abingdon was taken. It was this way that Colonel Gage made a heroic forced march south to rescue beleaguered Basing in 1644 and the safe base after Newbury. Faringdon, the other long-term royal base, was the home of the Pye family, but its Royalist owner found himself being attacked by his own son, Sir Robert Pye, who was Hampden's son in law. This Robert unwittingly helped the King's cause by presenting his father-in-law with a brace of pistols, one of which exploded and caused Hampden's mortal wound at Chalgrove Field.

Pye changed sides tactfully when Cromwell died and received favours from Charles II. Another Berks squire who stayed important throughout his life was John Wildman of Shrivenham, one of the few political thinkers Berkshire has produced. Originally a Leveller, then an advocate of Harrington's Commonwealth, he was very much a man who established his own practical version of government. He was an M.P., he was Postmaster General when that organisation was in its infancy . . . in fact, he ran it so efficiently that his enemies claimed he had a spy network, with provincial postmasters as a kind of Mafia. He was solicitor and friend of the second Duke of Buckingham, admired by Shaftesbury, disliked by Pepys, imprisoned by James II. In his time, he plotted against each King, and Cromwell too, always driven by his principles. All of them thought him important enough to conciliate, even to the end of his turbulent life. He was Alderman, Deputy Lieutenant for Middlesex and everyone's first choice for an active committee.

He was knighted in 1692, at sixty-nine, and died a year later.

He first married a Catholic Englefield, then the Anglican Lucy Lovelace of Hurley, which, for an agnostic, showed remarkable ecumenism. His only son, John, by the first wife, married a Shute and, dying childless, left Beckett Park and other estates to her kinsman, John Shute, Viscount Barrington, who continued the second name Wildman in his family out of gratitude.

The course of history was steered in 1714 by Lord Bolingbroke, who made sure that the Hanoverian elector was invited to the throne on the death of his distant cousin, Queen Anne, rather than letting the Stuart Pretender back to the throne. This choice brought about our present form of Parliamentary controlled monarchy, mainly because the good Elector, George I, couldn't speak English and gave up trying to understand what his ministers were doing. Bolingbroke was a Berkshire squire (among other things) since he had married Frances Winchcombe, heiress of Bucklebury and descendant of Jack of Newbury.

When they died childless, the manor went to the Packers, and through their heiress to the Hartleys and Hartley-Russells, who were content to enjoy their broad acres and leave politics to London men.

And this attitude was general in Berkshire—the local gentry stayed home, and nothing much happened. Some of them took an interest in the new-fangled ideas about farming current in Europe and it was one of these gentleman farmers who started a far more important revolution than any political one.

Jethro Tull

Jethro Tull, son of a small squire also named Jethro, during the Bible times of the Commonwealth, was born in 1674 at Basildon. He went to Oxford and trained as a lawyer, but came back in 1699 to the family estates at Sowberry Hall. Moving across to a farm near Shalbourne, he set out to make it pay. Seed in those days was sown by haphazard casting by hand from baskets. Jethro adapted the mechanism of organs to make a seed drill, which distributed with mechanical precision and increased his

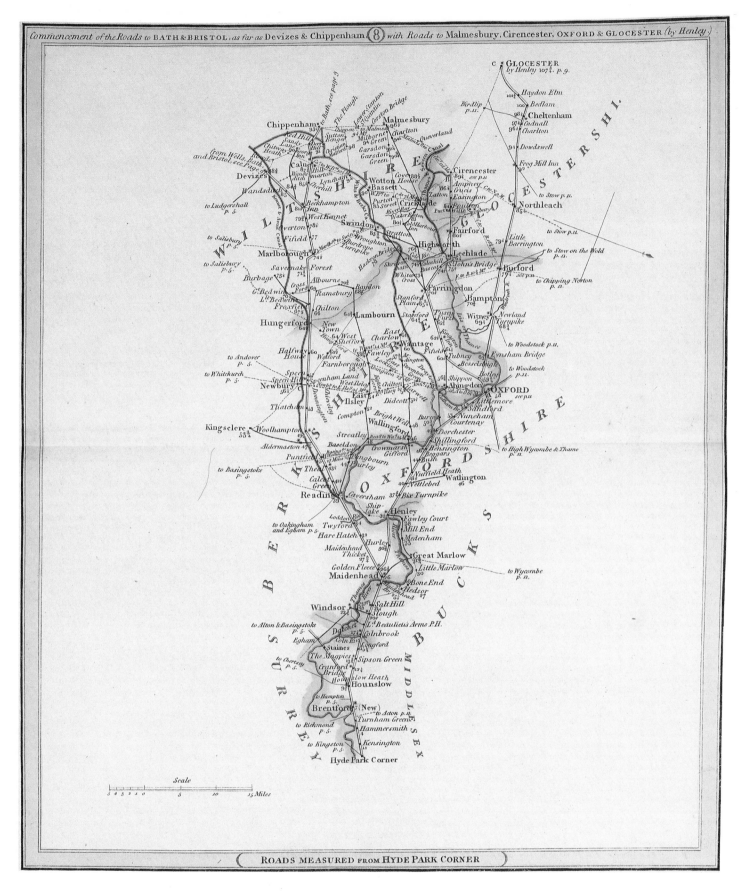

yields until his estate was nicknamed 'Prosperous Farm'. He studied French viticulture and came back full of enthusiasm for regular hoeing to keep weeds down—he wrote a book, *Horse Hoeing Husbandry*, which is a classic, though most of his ideas were opposed then, because they were new. Dust mulching, hoeing, mechanisation—all these enraged his neighbours and labourers, but they worked, so gradually other people began to try them. And this caused trouble.

Speenhamland and the Swing Riots

The Newbury suburb of Speenhamland is a dirty word to social historians because of what happened there in 1795 and caused great suffering to a large number of people all over the country.

There was growing agricultural poverty, partly because of current bad harvests but mostly because the new methods of agriculture required changes in the organisation of land-holding

xxiii

in the country. The old open fields had to go, but with the new 'enclosures' came great impoverishment of the former cottagers now degraded to the position of waged labourers only with no common rights to own and graze livestock. The new style farming required fewer total labourers just as the supply increased, so wages were depressed and few men could support their families without allowances from the parish.

A group of magistrates met in Speenhamland, with the avowed intention of fixing higher wages and standardising these parish allowances. They said vague things about free potatoes and fuel but, several drinks later, what emerged was only a basis for parish allowances—a man was to get the equivalent of 3 gallon loaves a week, plus 1½ loaves for a wife or children. This was intended to be a minimum but was adopted as a maximum and, for most labourers, reduced a wage. Later on, some Hampshire magistrates reduced the basic rate, but the name 'Speenhamland' stuck.

Desperate poverty was exacerbated by the gradual introduction of farm machinery, starting with the threshing machine, which took away autumn and winter work from the labourers. There was a lot of sympathy expressed by the upper classes, some of it even practically as charity and writers like William Cobbett rode around the country to get information and told Parliament about it. But no legislation was drawn up to help so in 1830 the labourers took matters into their own hands, smashing up machines and demanding fair wages, encouraged all the time by a mysterious writer 'Captain Swing' who issued threats of violence.

The Kintbury men were to the fore in this movement led by William Oakley, who kept strict discipline. Small risings in several villages brought the predictable reaction—all mobs were stopped with the full force of the law, including using the military, and most of the labourers were thrown into prison. They had destroyed property, demanded money with menaces and been cheeky to their betters. Special Commissions were set up to try these dangerous revolutionaries, including one at Reading. This was not half as vicious as the Hampshire one, partly because it sat later, and there had been a reaction in Parliament, and partly because the Reading justices were nicer people. The evidence in the various cases showed that some of the farmers and gentry had given a lot away in charity—Mr Mount of Wasing gave £100 to the local poor the previous winter, yet had his thresher smashed. Oakley, and two others, Alfred Darling (who had demanded a lot of money with menaces) and Winterbourne, another frequent leader, were sentenced to death. The latter was hung, the other two transported. Fifty-six Berkshire men tried at Reading were transported and thirty-six sent to prison for various terms—but this was mild compared with other counties. At Abingdon Assizes, forty-seven men were tried, but again, Mr Justice Park was comparatively lenient. One man, Thomas Mackrell, was transported and thirty-five sent to prison. Henry Woolridge was actually sentenced to death and must have thought himself very lucky to be imprisoned for eighteen months instead.

The gentry feared this was the prelude to a proper revolution, such as had happened that year in France. They arrested Cobbett, but not John Walter, whose *Times* had been as critical of the Government handling of the affair. Cobbett took the chance to make magnificent speeches and wipe the floor with the other side. This happened to be Denman, the prosecutor who had been most savage in his attacks on the poor labourers.

Nabobs and shopkeepers

Gradually, the old gentry families of Berkshire either died out in the male line or had to sell up as providing for large families took its toll. Then in came a new race of men whose income was not wholly derived from their landed estates. Some of these were 'nabobs', men who had made their fortunes as merchants with the East India company and whose sons often went back to their share of the pickings of the East. The Vansittart family made their money this way and bought a number of Berks estates including Bisham, Shottesbrooke, Clewer and Foxley from 1700 onwards, where they lived in almost Eastern splendour. London merchants, whom the local gentry sneered at as 'shopkeepers', also bought into landed estates and from the early 1800s, successful mill-owners from the north also moved in. These men mostly proved to be temporary residents whose only real interest in the county was to extract the maximum sporting amusement from it. They were the supporters of hunts, ruthless in maintaining rights of way, punishing those who poached to feed their children, even keeping rabbits and other wild prey as the preserve of the rich.

When they did settle down for a few years, they sometimes decided to contribute to local life in a way which could be seen by all like hiring an architect to 'restore' the church. The crimes inflicted on Berkshire churches in the name of restoration in the 1850s to 1870s stand as an indictment of architecture (and uneducated wealth) in those days.

Hungerford, being on the Bath road, seemed to attract political families. George Cherry of the Victualling Board bought Denford manor in the early nineteenth century and his family settled down to be local squires. Charles Dundas also bought property at Barton Court, and was Chairman of the notorious meeting of magistrates at Speenhamland in 1795. However, he was quite decent to the wretched labourers who were forced to revolt as a result, when he helped try their cases in 1830.

Another Scot who really enriched Berkshire by his residence, in both senses, was Robert Lindsay, of a noble but impoverished house, who married the enormously wealthy heiress of Lord Overstone, Harriet Loyd, in 1858. He was then a war hero with the V.C. to prove it, and might have spent his life hunting and trading on his past. However, he settled down at Lockinge House to run the estate prosperously and productively, while providing rewards for tenants and labourers in the form of primitive profit-sharing. He set up a co-operative shop at Ardington, brought unused land into cultivation, started a string of racehorses and a pedigree herd of cattle, built a reservoir, bought in a lot more local estates as they came on to the market and ran them for profit too. In his spare time he started the British Red Cross and founded University College, Reading, which always had a bias towards agriculture. This paragon, who was created Lord Wantage, died childless in 1901, and his widow in 1920, which split up again a magnificent estate.

One of the new squires who made an impression was John Elwes, the Miser. His paternal name was Meggot, and his father, George, was a brewer and M.P., who married Amy, sister of Hervey Elwes, a run-to-seed baronet. John Meggot inherited the estate and the surname and had a great fortune of his own which he used to purchase Marcham Park. Here he lived, on the absolute minimum which he could spend, and his only indulgence was hunting. At one period he kept fine horses and hounds but only the one servant to look after them, accompany him hunting, go home, feed the cows, get his master's meal and attend to the household chores, so that the total expenditure was less than £300 a year.

Elwes did have a mistress, whom he was too mean to marry, so that when he died all his entailed Elwes property went to his nephew, Richard Timms and Richard's son, John, who took the name Elwes. The Meggot share was left to the illegitimate sons, George and John Elwes of Marcham, and the younger was able to buy a Gloucestershire estate. George had only one daughter, Emily Elwes, who carried the Marcham property to her husband, Thomas Duffield. Their son inherited Marcham, but was childless so the inheritance was shared between his sisters, who married Head Pottinger Best of Donnington Grove (also a keen huntsman), John Phillips of Culham and Edwin Martin Atkins, whose family had bought Kingston Lisle manor from the Hydes in 1746.

The Duffields came into Berks through a lucky marriage with the heiress of Jeremiah Crutchley of Sunninghill Park, and Thomas's elder brother George adopted the name Crutchley on inheriting this property. At least there was a relationship here. The old Pusey family ended with Charles Pusey, who died in 1710, leaving the property to his sister's son, John Allen. John also died childless, leaving the estate to his sisters, who were somehow persuaded to hand it over to Philip Bouverie, who was a relative of John Allen's widow. Philip was the son of the second marriage of Jacob, Lord Folkestone, with older brothers

BERKSHIRE is upwards of 40 miles in length from east to west, and 30 in breadth from north to south. It is divided into 20 hundreds, which contain 12 market towns, 140 parishes, 21,195 houses; and its population amounts to 109,215.

This county, which is one of the most pleasant in England, is the summer residence of King George the Third. The soil is fertile, and produces great quantities of corn and timber. It carries on a great malting trade; and its principal manufactures are woollens and sail cloth. The chief rivers are the Thames and the Kennet.

An unusual circular map of Berkshire with a brief text comes from A New Pocket Atlas and Geography of England and Wales, illustrated with fifty-five copper plates showing the Great Post Roads with the Towns & Villages situated thereon by John Luffman, Geog.ʳ London, 1803. This miniature atlas—each map was about 60mm (2½in.) in diameter—was intended for children and was probably drawn originally for Luffman's own family. (By courtesy of the British Libary)

and nephews in plenty. He adopted the name Pusey, which his son hyphenated as Bouverie-Pusey. His younger son was Edward Bouverie-Pusey, the celebrated tract writer for the Oxford Movement.

Philip's elder half brother also picked up a Berks heiress, in Harriet Pleydell of Coleshill, and her father made it a condition of inheritance that his grandchildren should take the Pleydell name, hyphenated with Bouverie, and this is now the family name of the Earl of Radnor, a title they were given in 1765.

And so to Bath

From Roman times, Bath attracted people by its curative waters, and in the eighteenth century, when hypochondria was a way of life, a constant procession of rich invalids passed through Berkshire, in carriages and public stage coaches.

The roads were generally bad—not slightly potholed here and there by heavy lorries, but dirt roads, deformed by weather and pitted with huge ruts, in which a horse could break a leg and a coach lose a wheel. There was no metalling until Macadam became Surveyor of Roads in 1815. Before that, originally,

parishes collected baskets of stones from the fields and heaved them into the adjacent section of road. Later, the 'great roads' were taken over by Turnpike Trusts, which provided more systematic repair, for which the traveller paid in tolls. Even so, a coach journey west, jolting for three days over a bad surface in springless vehicles, was no casual undertaking.

Coaches ran from the 'Belle Sauvage' on Ludgate Hill, then the Saracen's Head in Cheapside, picking up in Piccadilly. They crossed Hounslow Heath, where the highwaymen jostled for their turn to rob a coach, and stopped at Colnbrook for breakfast, where two of the inns had grisly reputations for robbing and murdering passengers. The county was entered at Maidenhead bridge, after which came the hard pull up Knowle Hill, then through Twyford and Sonning to Reading, where everyone piled out for dinner in a choice of inns. If they felt peckish, a light tea might be had in summer at Theale or Woolhampton, and so on to Newbury, where the protesting bones of the traveller demanded an overnight stop.

Most Newbury inns were in the suburb of Speenhamland, clustered round the Pelican, the most expensive. Like the bird 'it was renowned for the size of its bill'. Apart from the important supper, Newbury offered attractions like theatrical entertainments—in a proper theatre too—which included not only plays but circus turns, spectacular shows, cockfighting and gambling.

In the morning, the bleary revellers faced the stiff climb from Chilton Foliat by Littlecote Park to Ramsbury, until an alternative road was built from Hungerford to Froxfield and across private Savernake Forest to Marlborough, which was easier on springs and tempers.

Coaching was an adventure, rather like an air flight now. Gentlemen vied to show their skills by taking over the reins for part of the journey, to the danger of the paying passengers. The driver was accompanied by a postillion, who sounded the horn to advise inns to have a change of horses and huge meals ready. He was also expected to defend the passengers against highwaymen—though sometimes postillions were in league with 'the gentlemen of the road'.

If two coaches met on the single width roadway, the lesser had to be lifted off the highway and on again, which is why gentlemen travelled with footmen for this task. Farm carters were often killed when their heavy vehicles rolled back over them as they struggled to get back on the highway when the gentry had passed.

Ordinary folk walked, travelled on horseback with saddlebags for their goods, or went by carrier's cart. These served a circuit of villages and the market town and carried a jumble of people, small livestock, boxes of goods and produce. If it rained, the goods were put under cover—people dried faster than a featherbed or roll of cloth!

The River road

The Thames formed the county boundary until 1974, and its drunken meanderings are responsible for the peculiar shape. The pattern of settlement was conditioned by it. Flooding and the threat of Danish raids made the banks unsafe in Saxon times. Later, settlements were established on the high side, but the river above Wallingford was not a practical trading route, except for local traffic. Poor road conditions made the effort necessary, especially for heavy or fragile goods, and the importance of Oxford required goods to be carried there. They were mostly off-loaded at Wallingford or Shillingford on to carts, for Abingdon's low bridge was intended for road, not barge traffic.

The Thames proper started at Dorchester, where the Thames met the Isis. Probably the original head water *was* the Thame, but some early geographer in London picked the longest possible route, to make the capital's river seem grander. It is the Isis which straggles across from Lechlade, joined by the Cherwell at Oxford, the Ock at Abingdon and the Thame, then becoming Tame-isis. At Reading they are joined by the Kennet, a useful river with tributaries of its own in the Enbourne and Lambourne streams. The Loddon enters the Thames at Wargrave.

Mills were set up, especially on the amiable Ock, and water

WINDSOR CASTLE
from the Little Park.

Berkshire by Christopher and John Greenwood, 1824

Christopher Greenwood (1786–1855) began preparing a series of large-scale maps of all the English counties in 1817. The Ordnance Survey, founded in 1791, was progressing so slowly that there was still a market for private mapping ventures and public demand for up-to-date maps. Greenwood's series began well, but, where the official survey was financed by the Government, Greenwood depended on subscriptions. Eventually, his project was overtaken by competition from the Ordnance Survey and from other publishers. Several jumped on the bandwagon, producing individual county maps before Greenwood's were ready, and there were underhand manœuvres to win over subscribers. Only thirty-five of the forty-one maps were completed. The series was abandoned in 1831 and the Greenwood firm collapsed soon after.

Christopher Greenwood, a Yorkshireman, established himself in London in 1818 and his brother John (fl.1821-40) became his partner in 1821. The all-important financial side was handled by George Pringle and his son, also George. Some of the work for their maps was taken from the Ordnance Survey and other sources, but a large part was original. Parish boundaries, for instance, were included by the Greenwoods, but this was a mixed blessing as they were often disputed. The recorded costing of the surveys was remarkably low and this may be reflected in some inaccuracies through hurried work done on the cheap.

A section of a "Map of the Berks from an Actual Survey made in the years 1822 & 1823" shows the Greenwoods' distinctive style. Their maps are finely engraved, each with a large vignette view and decorative title and on a scale of one-inch to the mile. At this period enclosing of land and new farming techniques had made grain-growing and milling particularly important in the country, and the Greenwoods detailed both watermills and windmills. They also marked some industrial sites, such as paper mills and brick kilns, as well as the more usual archaeological remains, private estates and parkland. Though their maps were gradually superseded by the Ordnance Survey, which set a new standard of accuracy, they contain a large amount of information on early nineteenth century England and several were still being issued in the 1860s. (By courtesy of the British Library)

power harnessed. Later river management channelled and embanked the river, making a few short cuts across the most outrageous bends. From time to time, Father Thames took his revenge, boiling floodwater along the river and, because the old water meadows left to accommodate floods had gone, invading the towns and villages on the 'safe' side.

Above Oxford, the Isis has never been a serious river for transport. Farmers, and the occasional traveller, crossed by ferry or took cows a couple of miles in small boats. Robert de Vere, fleeing from the battle of Radcot Bridge, threw off his armour and swam for it, and escaped to obscurity in France. Generations of Oxford students have followed his example, rowing off up river to swim or enjoy an orgy in 'the stripling Thames at Bablockhythe' or elsewhere. The fascinations of exploring twisting backwaters and pitting muscle against wayward currents made the Thames a pleasure resort.

The young men and their elders enjoyed angling, the patient pursuit of the wily pike or wriggling chub with rod and line. There had always been fishing and even commercial fishery ponds, mainly in the broader reaches. Boat builders learned to make special boats with an open 'keep tank' in the centre, so that the smaller fish could be admired and thrown back, to fight another day. In the late nineteenth century, the fisheries were spoiled by the effluent from the Reading and other factories. Mills were worked by steam and the once flourishing craft of paper making moved elsewhere. Osier beds, grown for basket making, languished. The river ceased to be a workhorse and became a plaything for the middle classes. Boating parties became the rage, with banjo accompaniment, at first in rowing or sailing boats, then steamers. Riverside inns formerly patronised by locals and a few students metamorphosed into hotels with enormous tea-gardens, riverside stalls and games. The social spectrum widened later and jellied eel stalls were to be found. First the phonograph, then the gramophone, disturbed the nesting birds.

Riverside houses were fashionable. Sir George Young, a former Admiral, got in early at Cookham, by towing an old ship upstream and using the timbers to build a house called *The Formosa*. A backwater and private boathouse were fine, until trippers came and parked on your lawn. A later Lady Young spent her summers attacking the moored pleasure boats!

The great 'tourist centres' were below Wallingford—Maidenhead, Cookham, Pangbourne and the honeypots, like Henley Regatta, Boulter's Lock, Skindle's, and Monkey Island at Bray. Locks were natural places for tourists, and there hotels and entertainments proliferated—even the lock-keepers sometimes ran tea-gardens. The tangle of punts, canoes, steamers and later motorboats, inexpertly handled, made the river potentially dangerous, though there were always possible rescuers around. Floods usually came in winter, when the tourists had gone home—they were very bad in 1897 and 1903.

The new activity necessitated more locks and 'cuts' and the raising or replacing of old, low bridges, intended for road transport. Maidenhead Bridge was the most important, since it carried the Bath road. Edward I's queen left money for it, and later grants allowed wood to be taken from Windsor Forest for its repair. Wallingford Bridge, which had carried the second main road west, was much less important after Bessels and Barbour had the new Abingdon bridges built in 1416.

In other places, a ferry, then a footbridge, then a road bridge, formed the crossing, and as traffic increased, the bridges soon needed widening and strengthening. Marlow Bridge, with footings on marshy land, was closed on and off for decades. Caversham Bridge could not be closed even for a short time for widening, so a second (Reading) bridge was built a couple of hundred yards away. With provision for railways and cars, the river was soon laced with crossing points, some more attractive and/or functional than others.

The car soon relieved the pressure on the river, by enabling people to get to the seaside—otherwise, the Thames would have been choked from bank to bank with pleasure craft. There is still plenty of activity in summer, either organised Regattas and races or 'just messing about in boats.'

The Canal era

As barges increased in size, the natural courses of rivers were inadequate to carry them—apart from the fact that nature did not necessarily have an eye to the best trading routes.

The Wilts and Berks Canal was built in 1801, and started in Abingdon, where it connected with the Thames and thence to Oxford and its canal to the Midlands. It ran south-west, by Wantage and Uffington to Swindon and Chippenham, or nearby. Because canal construction was still a matter of brute force and some ignorance, the course wandered rather, almost as badly as a river in places, and it missed the towns.

The other major canal, the Kennet and Avon, was better laid out. It rain at first from Midgham, the furthest easily navigable place on the Kennet, sticking closely to the course of the river, where nature had for once done a good job, until Hungerford, when it cut south west through the Vale of Pewsey to Devizes and Bradford on Avon. Here it met that river and was connected with Bristol. The Wilts and Berks turned south to meet the Kennet and Avon near Melksham. The great bulk of the White Horse Hills lay between for much of the length of the two canals, and prevented a direct link from Abingdon or Wantage south to the Kennet.

Once the second canal was built, the first started to decline since better access to the west could be had by Kennet. Even farmers in the Vale of the White Horse would cart to Sutton Courtenay or Wallingford and send their produce to Reading, from whence it could go more rapidly than by the Wilts and Berks. The coming of the railways hammered the last nail in the coffin, at least in the Berkshire section, and the canal was drained or left to silt up by the end of the nineteenth century.

Ascot Race Course by Edward Mogg, 1829

Horse racing has been a major sport in Berkshire for centuries and, with Windsor Castle in the county, it has always been closely associated with Royalty. There were courses near most of the main towns, but it is the Ascot season that has become important in the social calendar. Though races on nearby Datchet Mead were appointed by Charles II, Queen Anne founded the Ascot Course and the first race was run there in August 1711. It gained in popularity under the Duke of Cumberland who donated the Gold Cup in 1807. By this time, Ascot was already a place where one had to be seen and where the latest fashions should be worn. With the Prince Regent – later George IV – the social importance of Ascot Week was established. The Royal Drive was instituted and the course extended and improved. Edward Mogg's "Plan of Ascot Race Course, Surveyed in 1829" shows "all the improvements lately executed by Command of His Majesty". He also lists the races and, in fact, "all the information requisite for Gentlemen of the Turf and visitors in general".

Edward Mogg's publications span the first half of the nineteenth century, providing maps for the traveller and tourist. From premises, first in the Covent Garden area of London and later from Blooms-bury, he produced a stream of maps and atlases – and advice for travellers – on roads, railways, steamships, London and its environs. He made a name for himself with a series of maps informing the public of the correct fares to be charged by cab-drivers. Not surprisingly, he was unpopular with the cabbies. Perhaps it indicates that Ascot had "arrived" as a public occasion when a shrewd, successful publisher such as Mogg feels it worthwhile printing a map of the course. (By courtesy of the British Library).

The Railways

The Great Western Railway, under Isambard Kingdom Brunel, was built as a seven foot gauge line from London to Bristol, starting in 1833 and opened in 1841. This followed the Great West road from Maidenhead to Reading then curved north west to Pangbourne, crossed the Thames to Goring, and back again to Moulsford, towards Didcot, through the Vale of the White Horse to Swindon. Later, the line had to be converted to the standard gauge which was what everyone else used.

Branch lines were built from Reading to Basingstoke in Hampshire and west to Hungerford along the Kennet valley, taking much the same course as the canal. Later in the century this was continued along the Vale of Pewsey—precisely the canal course, but for the time being, the canal got some extra business west from Hungerford. Hard-headed Berkshire farmers realised that canals were slower, but much cheaper than the railways, so the Kennet and Avon managed to keep going.

Short branch lines were built from Maidenhead to High Wycombe, from Twyford to Henley and Windsor was reached by a short line from Slough, before the railway entered Berkshire. Queen Victoria thought rail travel was great fun, and had her own carriage, elaborately furnished, like a palace on wheels.

The next important connection intended was the Oxford line, proposed to go through Abingdon, where the engineering works would be placed. Resistance by Abingdon councillors, who were canal men, forced the building of a line across river loops and marshy land via Radley. This line diverted freight from the Wilts and Berks canal until it was forced to close. Too late, Abingdon realised their commercial mistake, and got a push-pull branch line from Radley station, but this was never very convenient and Abingdon lost a great deal of trade and influence. Wallingford, also by-passed, later got a branch line from Cholsey, and maintained its status as a depot for corn, sent by river to Reading. It also benefitted from the new tourism.

Didcot grew from tiny village to unlovely junction town, dominated by the marshalling yards to the north. It shared with Swindon the new engineering works. New connections were made from Didcot through Newbury to Hampshire and a 'horse-box' line down the Lambourne valley was built, but these

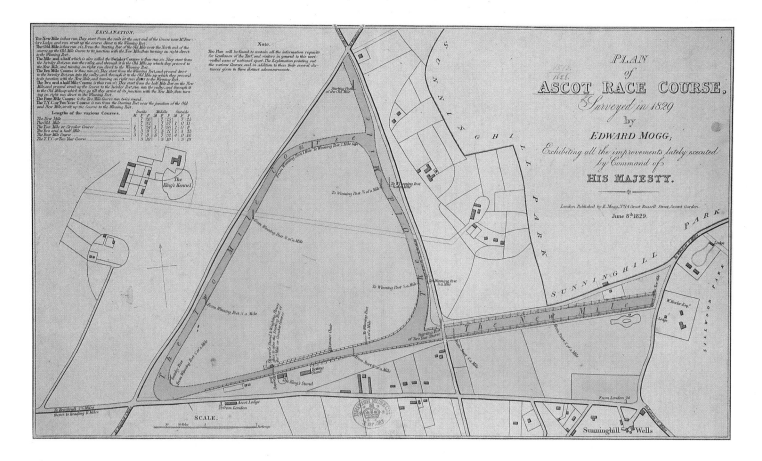

are now disused. The existence of good trains to Didcot junction undoubtedly conditioned the siting of AERE Harwell nearby.

The main line west from Didcot misses the towns and villages by two or three miles, in an effort to serve two places at once. Formerly people had a long walk or cart ride to Wantage road, Challow road and Uffington road, from these villages plus Stanford in the Vale, East Hanney and Faringdon. Faringdon folk, with six miles to go, demanded a branch line of their own.

Reading was also a junction town—in fact, its northern area near the Thames was choked with tracks, when the later line to Wokingham and Ascot was added to the main and southern branch lines.

Racing and Chasing

The Berkshire Downs are not good agricultural country, but there were and are great expanses of thin grassland, where the soil is not deep enough for normal cultivation but is ideal for the production of turf whose roots mat close to the surface and produce a springy, firm surface—the perfect going for horses. However, chance rather than scientific choice probably contributed more to the proliferation of racing stables on the Downs.

William, Duke of Cumberland, son of George II, is infamous as the 'Butcher of Culloden', when he wiped out the flower of Scottish clansmen with total ruthlessness after the 1745 Rebellion. When you have been commander in chief of the Army, and scored such a resounding victory at twenty-three, peacetime life seems a little dull. The Duke settled into bachelor quarters at Gore Hill in East Ilsley and found a new interest, the breeding of bloodstock. Attempts had been made before to improve the English horse by crossing it with Arabian or Barbary steeds imported for the purpose. In 1748 the Duke put his favourite mare, *Cypron*, to the stallion *Tartar*, descended from the famous *Byerley Turk*, one of these imports, and produced *King Herod*, a fine racehorse. *Herod* sired excellent stock, including the fabulous *Highflyer*, though some of them had a tendency to burst blood vessels under pressure.

In 1764, the Duke produced a legend, *Eclipse*. He had exchanged an Arab of his own for a cross-bred Yorkshire colt, *Marske*, descended from the Darley Arabian and other Eastern horses, including Lord Fairfax's *Moroccan* and another mare of impeccable Eastern descent known unromantically as *Old Bald Peg*. *Marske* and the moderately well-descended mare, *Spiletta*, produced the colt *Eclipse*, so named because he was born during one, in 1764. William died in 1765 and his stable was sold up. *Marske* and *Eclipse* were brought at third-hand by a meat salesman named William Wildman, who spotted their potential. *Marske* cost 20 guineas and was shortly sold for 1000 gns to Lord Abingdon, for whom he proved an exceptional sire.

In those days horses were not raced until they were four, but even so *Eclipse* won ten races and had countless 'walk-overs' in his two-year career. He then settled down to sire progeny, who were later crossed with *Herod* stock to produce champions. *Eclipse* was never beaten—his part-owner, Dennis O'Kelly, coined the phrase 'Eclipse first, the rest nowhere' to describe the contemptuous ease with which he strode away from the rest. O'Kelly made £25,000 in stud fees between 1770 and 1788, apart from betting income, and Wildman a lot more.

Racing really started at Newmarket and in Yorkshire but as it was a favourite sport of the royal family, they brought it with them to Windsor, at first using Datchet Mead but later establishing a proper racecourse at Ascot. Queen Anne instituted the Queen's Plate, prize 100 guineas, in 1711, run for on 11 August, and regular races took place in August from 1713, over the same Ascot course. The Duke of Cumberland increased the meetings to twice a year in May/June and August/September in 1753.

Because of its early associations with the Court, Ascot has always been a great social occasion, where the racegoers are divided into separate enclosures, to which admittance was strictly by good birth (or extreme wealth). Until recently, divorced persons were not admitted to a Royal enclosure and a public scandal was enough to lose the entree. To the first race in 1711, Miss Forrester, a maid of honour, went in men's clothing. More recently, women's fashion has dictated often unsuitable party flimsies and elaborate eye-catching, wind-catching hats, instead of the more practical clothes often called for by an English June. The Royal family, keen racegoers for centuries, arrive in a carriage procession down the course from Windsor Castle, watched by many less knowledgeable punters.

Abingdon corporation set up a town race course in 1733 at Culham Heath and funded a Plate valued at £10, later increased to £50. By 1800, there was opposition to this misuse of the rates and the course declined until it was closed in 1875. Reading had a course from 1747, but it could not challenge Ascot and was closed in 1873. Newbury built a course on the Wash, in 1749, then transferred it to Enborne Heath, with a Corporation Plate worth £50. After the high point in 1815, when a Gold Cup worth £100 was competed for, the course declined to a close, but was reopened in 1905 under the management of the trainer, John Porter. There were also occasional meetings at Maidenhead Thicket and in Ilsley and more recently in Windsor itself.

It is small wonder that there were racing stables to serve the courses at Lambourne, Childrey, Ilsley, Compton, Whitcombe, Letcombe Regis and other villages. Some were set up and run by gentlemen interested in the breeding first and the winning of races second. Some were run by commercial breeders intending to sell their horses to the gentry. Some were set up by super-annuated jockeys, or sometimes by ex-cavalry officers, who trained horses to win races usually for more than one owner at a time.

The chance of winning a lot of money for nothing has attrac-ted many men over the centuries and attempts to manipulate the results encouraged a doubtfully honest fringe. Many people have become compulsive gamblers and diverted money which belonged to their children. However, the kind of betting talk which can be overheard in Berkshire pubs, between small wiry men who have known the animals they are backing since they were a gleam in the stallion's eye, is a different matter. Racing has brought nothing but prosperity to the majority of Berkshire people involved.

The enthusiasm for equine blood-lines extends to people. In Letcombe Regis, the 'local' proudly displays the pedigree of champion jockey Lester Piggot, from the jockey-trainer family of Day, via Tom Cannon, the jockey, father of Morny and Kemp-ton Cannon, Derby winners, and jump jockey Ernest Piggot to trainer Keith Piggot (who lives locally), his wife, a Rickaby, and Lester himself. Charles 'Jimmy' Blunt was, until a couple of years ago, a trainer in Letcombe and his ending is remembered locally. He refused to make his final journey in a hearse, preferring instead the removal van of a local firm, which happened to be in his racing colours of claret and cream.

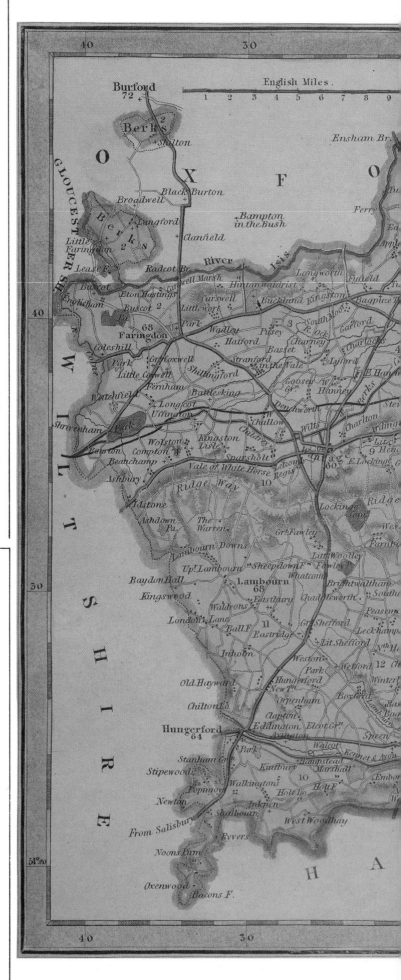

Berkshire by Archibald Fullarton & Co., 1843

The Great Western Railway appears on Archibald Fullarton & Co.'s "Berkshire" from The Parliamentary Gazetteer of England *and* Wales *(1843). Isambard Kingdom Brunel's "finest work in England"—as he enthusiastically called it—had been the brain-child of a group of Bristol businessmen keen to build a fast link between London and the western port. After two years of legal battling, the new railway Bill was passed in 1835 and work began. There were challenges to Brunel's engineering skill in constructing the line across eastern Berkshire. A new bridge at Maidenhead, with the longest, flattest arches ever attempted in brickwork, had problems at first, but defied its critics by standing up to the weight of the trains. A two-mile cutting at Sonning Hill had to be worked in appalling conditions during an abnormally wet winter. After Sonning, the going was easier. The first train steamed as far as Reading in March 1840 and by July a temporary terminus was built at Challow near White Horse Vale. In June 1841, the line was open through to Bristol.*

Gazetteers and popular atlases were a speciality of Archibald Fullarton & Co. (fl.1834–50). The firm started in Glasgow, expanding to Edinburgh and London in 1843 and Dublin in 1845. Between 1833 and 1837 they published the four volumes of James Bell's A New and Comprehensive Gazetteer of England and Wales. *It was illustrated with forty-four maps, including the individual English counties, each adorned with an attractive vignette view. These were re-used in* The Parliamentary Gazet-teer *about ten years later, updated only by the addition of the railway lines. However, the new Gazetteer was successful and ran to several editions in the 1840s. (By courtesy of Robert Douwma Prints and Maps Ltd)*

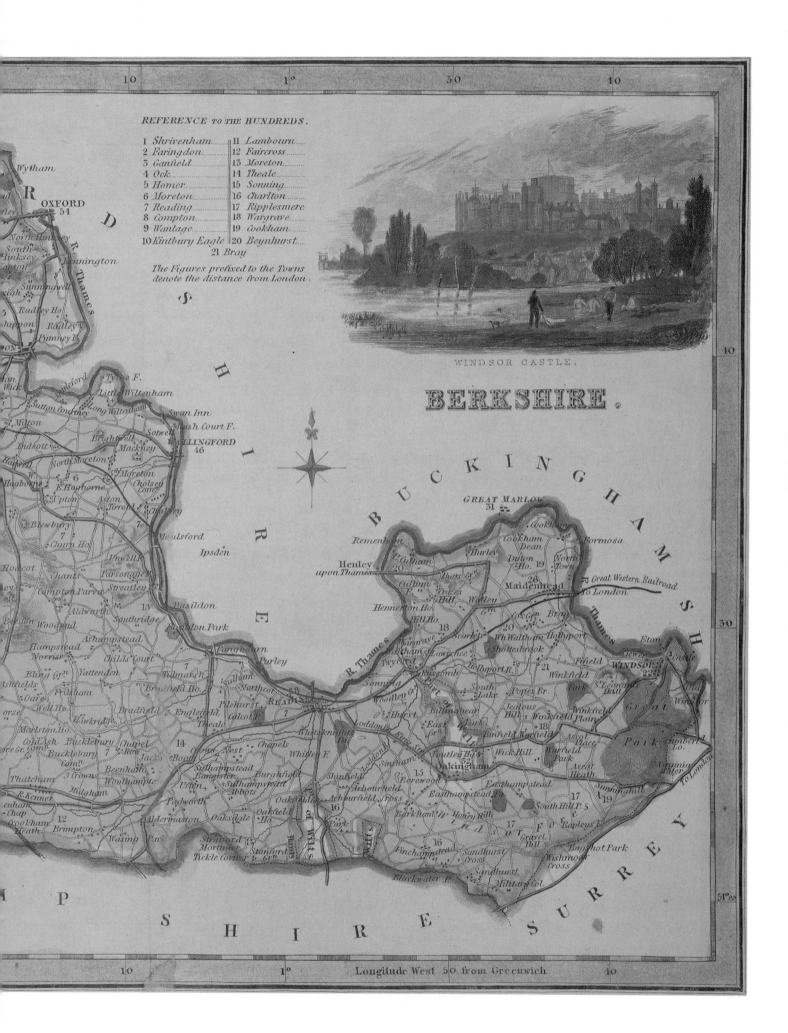

Hunting and Harrying

In medieval times, most cattle had to be killed off in winter and it was important to supplement the diet with whatever came to hand, or bow. Stags were abundant and their meat made a tasty addition to salt pork or salt beef (or, for the lucky coast dweller, salt fish). Chasing and killing was fun, so it was reserved for the local lord, but his people got the ample left-overs, which could not be stored.

As time went on, there was less connection between hunting and food provision and more emphasis on sheer volume of the kill, which was the yardstick for 'good sport'. Stags rapidly ran out and had to be imported to the hunt area from elsewhere.

The Royal family kept a pack of Buckhounds at Windsor and the chase was popular even with Queen Anne, George III and George IV, though they were much too heavy to ride, so had to follow in carriages. This accounts for the broad 'rides' in Windsor Great Park. Private packs were kept by men like the eccentric Lord Barrymore, whose carted stags had been kept as pets, and nuzzled up to the horses instead of running away. Sir Robert Wilmot of Binfield converted a pack of harriers into the Berks and Bucks farmers' Staghounds, to cater for the gentleman farmer. Seymour Dubourg kept a stag-hunting pack as late as 1880, with carted prey, and had permission to hunt in Windsor Great Park.

Fox hunting mostly took over as stags vanished, and the Old Berkeley at first included Berks in their territory, hunting four days a week across country, mainly on gentry estates, whose farmer tenants dare not object. Well known gentlemen who were Masters of hunts from time to time included John Elwes the Miser, Lord Craven, William Thoyts of Sulhamsted, Thomas Smith, Head Pottinger Best, Stephen Poyntz of Thatcham, the sporting parson, Henry Ellis St John, Sir John Cope, J.J. Wheble of Bulmershe, T.C. Garth and John Hargreaves of Maiden Erleigh. Their huntsmen, who actually bred and cared for the packs, included members of the Bartlett, Sweetman, Tocock, King, Goodall and Harvey families.

Former 'sports' which were popular with our ancestors, who did not think of the cruelty involved, were bear-baiting and cock-fighting. Fox hunting and hare coursing still survive amidst some controversy. The attractive aspects of dressing up and comparing riding skills are now catered for by eventing and gymkhanas, increasingly popular in recent years. The royal family give a lead in these fields as they once did with stag-hunting.

And as a footnote, Berkshire must have one of the earliest recorded examples of football violence. In 1598, John and Richard Gregory were buried at North Moreton and the register notes:—

'These two men were killed by Ould Gunter. Gunter's soones and ye Gregories fell together by ye yeares at footeball. Ould Gunter drew his dagger and broke boothe their heades and they died boothe within a fortnight after.'

Ten years later, the Guners and Gregorys were at it again when a Gunter accused several Gregory women of bewitching her, thus demonstrating the way sports disputes can escalate. At least this one cannot be blamed on the media, since the *Reading Mercury* did not start until 1723, and the *Berkshire Chronicle* until the 1770s.

The Pen is mightier

Only a few of Berkshire's literary men are native sons—most moved in for health reasons, or when success allowed the purchase of an estate.

Elias Ashmole (1617–92) wrote extensive notes during his period as Windsor Herald, published long after his death as *The History and Antiquities of the County of Berkshire*. He had a talent for marrying well, to support his studies, and founded the Ashmolean Museum with the collections of himself and his friend, John Tradescant. Thomas Hearne, born in 1678 in Littlefield Green, also studied Berks antiquities, mostly after his move to Oxford as Deputy Keeper of the Bodleian Library.

Alexander Pope (1688–1744) was born in London, but his parents brought him to Binfield for his health. His early work was written there, including his translation of the *Odyssey*. A

local tutor, Elijah Fenton, claimed that much of the translation was his work, not Pope's, but this was never acknowledged, though probably true.

Also in Binfield lived Mrs Catherine Macaulay, whose celebrated eight volume *History of England* came out from 1764. Pitt praised it, Mirabeau translated it, George Washington read it and feted her. Dr Johnson was the one carper—he liked his women adoring and stupid. A rash second marriage alienated all her male admirers.

Mary Russell Mitford (1787–1855) was brought to Berkshire by her father, Dr George Mitford, a compulsive gambler, when a lottery ticket in her name won £20,000. At least she got a decent education out of it, before he lost the lot and they had to move to a labourer's cottage in Three Mile Cross. Her writing of plays, poems, essays—anything saleable—kept them going till his merciful death enabled her to live in comfort. She is best remembered for *Our Village* and her *Recollections*, based on chatty letters to friends.

Pangbourne was the home of Thomas Morton (1764–1838) the playwright, whose one memorable character is Mrs Grundy, in *Speed The Plough*, who never appears, but is constantly mentioned—'What will Mrs Grundy say?'

John Walter, the coal merchant who started a newspaper, *The Universal Register,* in 1785 (which became *The Times* in 1788) was originally interested in the use of steam power, which his son, John II, actually applied to the printing presses in 1814. John II could set type and print himself, and so beat a compositors' strike. The family bought Bear Wood, near Reading and lived there for some generations.

John Newbury, contemporary of John Walter I, published children's books, now sought after in the sale room. His *Universal Chronicle* published Johnson's *Idler* essays, and he had the doubtful honour of being the friend and subsidiser of Oliver Goldsmith. He started work on the *Mercury* at Reading, which is half a century older than *The Times*.

Charles Knight, born in Windsor, was a prolific publisher and his fascinating history of London, published in parts from 1841, is an entertaining yet scholarly work. He was a social reformer too and had great influence.

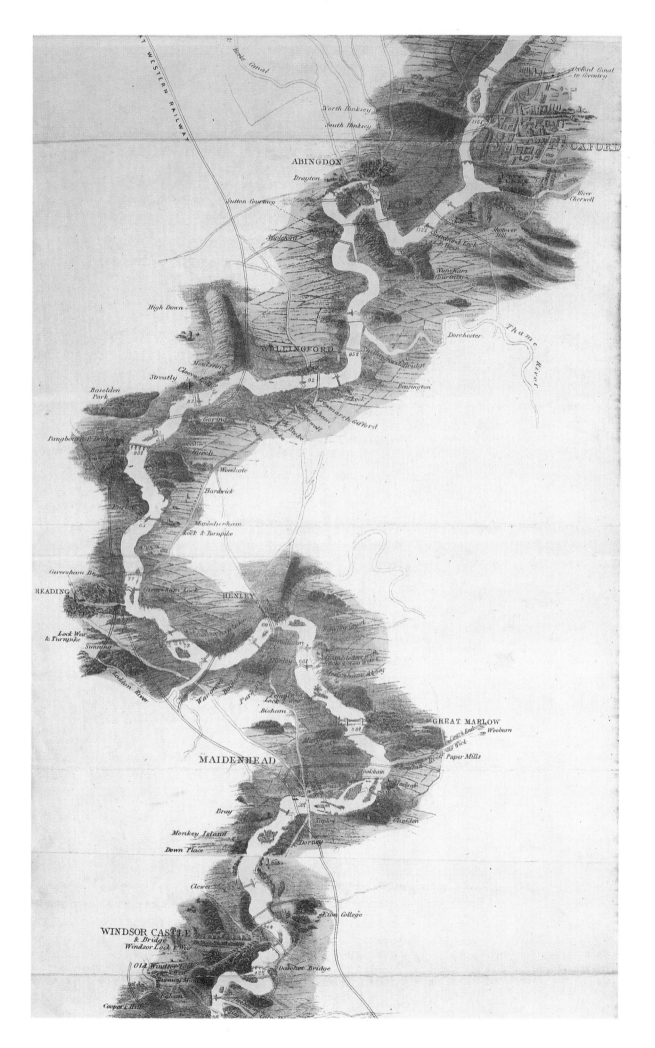

A century later, Kenneth Grahame, former Bank of England official, wrote his one work, *The Wind in the Willows* for his son at Cookham Dean, and later he too lived in Pangbourne. This anthropomorphic story of Mole, Ratty and Toad has been turned into a play which is performed regularly and admired by adults as well as children.

Charles Kingsley, renowned as author of another children's classic, *The Water Babies*, lived for some time near Lambourne, and that town (with a few facets of Newbury) is thought to have been the model for 'Whitbury' in *Twenty Seven Years After* (1857).

R.D. Blackmore, later author of *Lorna Doone*, grew up in Longworth, where his father was vicar. An earlier son of a vicar there, John Fell, has gone down in literature as a character, rather than a writer. He was Dean of Christchurch, and set an unruly student some 'lines', which involved translating a Martial epigram. The result was:

> I do not love thee, Doctor Fell,
> The reasons why, I cannot tell;
> But this I know, and know full well:
> I do not l love thee, Doctor Fell.

Thomas Day, who lived at Bear Place, Wargrave, wrote a boys' story, *Sandford and Merton*, which is impeccably moral, but very dull. His ideals were so high that no woman could match them, so he acquired two female orphans whom he proposed to train up in his own philosophies, then select one as a wife. However, they did not match up to expectations, so he married them off and found himself an heiress, who was slightly odd but very rich, and turned his attention to the training of ideal horses, by kindness alone. Unfortunately, a wild colt which had not read the manual threw him and killed him.

Berks gave a home to Shelley briefly but he found Bracknell so unstimulating that he spent the time sailing paper boats instead of writing. Henry Pye, Poet Laureate to George III, was born in Faringdon, scion of the local gentry family, but although he wrote a great deal, it is best forgotten. Walter Scott visited Sunninghill regularly (and wrote about Cumnor). Mrs Montague of Sandelford Priory near Newbury entertained there her 'Bluestockings' and all the leading literary lions of the day, including the ungrateful Johnson.

All the northern district near Oxford has association with Matthew Arnold, whose *Scholar Gipsy* roamed the Cumnor Hills and is full of quotations about the Fyfield Elm, the 'stripling Thames at Bablockhythe' and 'the lone alehouses on the Berkshire moors'.

His exact contemporary, Thomas Hughes (1822–96), went to Rugby School, run by Matthew's father, Dr Thomas Arnold, and crystallised the experience in the most famous school story of them all, *Tom Brown's Schooldays*, which provided a pattern of expectation for future public schools. Tom was the son of John Hughes of Donnington Priory, himself author in 1830 of the *Boscobel Tracts*, and Tom Brown, like Tom Hughes, 'dwelt in the Vale of the White Horse'. The first three chapters of the book are an excellent picture of life in the 1830s in the Uffington area.

Hughes wrote *Tom Brown* in 1857 (the same year when Matthew Arnold was writing his equally laudatory but much less readable poem, *Rugby Chapel*). He was by then a barrister and later became a County Court judge, despite being a Christian Socialist and introducing Trade Union legislation into Parliament while he was an M.P.

One of his other books was *The Scouring of the White Horse* (1859), which celebrates an occasional event when the local people combine to strip grass and weeds off the lines of the Old Horse. Nowadays, Boy Scouts tend to have a corner on this sort of exercise—then everyone joined in, because the local gentry provided unlimited beer to participants.

The saddest association of an author and Berkshire is, perhaps, that Oscar Wilde spent two years in Reading prison after he tangled with the savage Marquess of Queensberry, father of his one-time good friend, Lord Alfred Douglas. The result was his exile and death, within a few years—and the powerful *Ballad of Reading Goal*, published in 1898, which brings home the sheer terror and pity of his situation.

Scientia Docet

There is something in the air of Berkshire which brings out the scientist in people, or attracts those who are involved in science and technology.

John Blagrave, the Reading mathematician, was of a local gentry family as was Samuel Morland (1625–95) of Sulhamstead Bannister who invented a speaking trumpet, intended for sea-captains to give orders in a storm. He also invented a calculating machine, which Pepys nastily described as 'very pretty but not useful', water pumps and engines which fascinated Charles II and a set of tables for simple and compound interest, for Restoration insurance agents.

Edmund Dickinson of Appleton was court physician to Charles II, who showed that his interest in science was genuine by letting Edmund set up a laboratory under the royal bedchamber, which may have startled the royal mistresses at times. John Evelyn reports him as 'very learned, old and infirm, yet continuing chemistry'.

David Gregory, astronomer friend of Isaac Newton, is buried at Maidenhead, so is William Lassells, the irritating Lancashire mechanic who made his own lenses, superbly, and was able to see further than and therefore correct the fashionable astronomer, Herschel. Francis Baily, born in the 1770s in Newbury, was also an astronomer, and his observations on eclipses have immortalised his name. 'Baily's beads' occur as the sun disappears and reappears.

The modern Atomic Energy Research Establishment, though actually located at Chilton, where its tangle of labs and outbuildings sprawl beside the road, had also changed the character of Harwell, which is its official address, which is now a dormitory village instead of a mass of cherry orchards. One grower's fields, with their neat rows of shortened trees, still give an idea of what it was like in springtime. The similar AERE buildings at Aldermaston centred on the old manor house, used to be the starting point for an annual Easter protest march into London.

Aldermaston contributed something of more lasting value to humanity almost two centuries ago when the local schoolmaster, an enthusiastic horticulturalist, produced the juicy Aldermaston cross or William Pear. Across the county at Longworth his contemporaries were bending their energies to producing the perfect rose and varieties like the *Bardou Job* and *Reve d'Or* bloomed here.

Schools

Education of children was always part of the functions of a religious foundation and Abingdon Abbey had sufficient reputation to attract William I. Reading no doubt started to educate the children of barons and the richest merchants soon after its founding in 1121. This association of the church and education continued right through the centuries since it was customary for the parish clergy to make extra money by teaching local children and taking in a few boarding pupils, especially from the late eighteenth century, the children of parents employed in India or other parts of the Empire.

Secular education developed as a protest against the hold of these two Abbeys (and other smaller foundations) over the trading life of the town. Merchants in violent dispute would not send their sons to the monks so they employed schoolmasters of their own. Gradually these alternatives evolved into town Grammar Schools, in Reading and Abingdon, though the precise dates are uncertain.

Officially, Reading School was founded by Henry VII in 1486, no doubt building on an existing group as a counter to the

This informative guide to the river is a section of E.G. Ravenstein's "The Oarsman's and Angler's Map of the River Thames" (1861), which was published in London by James Reynolds. (By courtesy of the British Library)

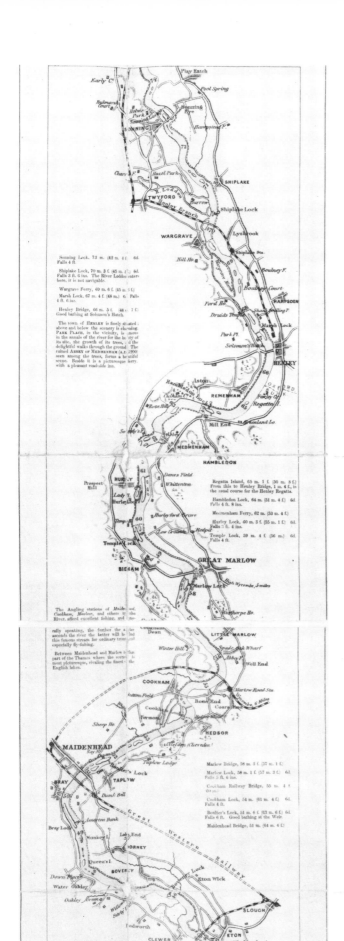

Abbey which had supported his enemies. Its most famous pupil was William Laud (1573–1645), who went on to St John's College Oxford (founded by Sir Thomas White, another Reading Grammar boy), entered the church and progressed steadily upwards, through Archdeacon, Dean, Prebendary and Bishop to being Archbishop of Canterbury, in 1633. He was strictly a High Churchman, in a period when very many clergymen were toying with Puritanism and he had a little list, with 'O' against the name of the Orthodox and 'P' against the Puritans, who got no preferment while he was in charge. His uncompromising opposition to reform led to a head on confrontation with the Scots Presbyterians, which turned into a disastrous war. Laud was made the scapegoat, indicted for high treason and executed.

Other pupils included John Blagrave, a famous mathematician in Tudor times; White, who also founded Merchant Taylor's school; Judge Talfourd, friend of Wordsworth, to whom Dickens dedicated *Pickwick Papers*; and Dr Lempriere, whose *Classical Dictionary* inspired Keats and was once a standard reference book. Reading had two notable headmasters. One, Jocelyn Palmer, was burnt as a Protestant at Newbury in 1556. The other, Dr Richard Valpy, was renowned as a flogger in an age when 'spare the rod, spoil the child' was the eleventh commandment, and remained at Reading for fifty years, even when offered a bishopric.

Reading also had a Bluecoat School for boys and a Greencoat School for girls, both dating from the early 1600s. The latter is surprising for our ancestors did not believe in educating females.

Abingdon's Grammar School was long in existence when John Roysse, local boy made good as a merchant in London, left ample money for restoration in 1563. The school has a special relationship with Pembroke College, founded by Abingdon man Thomas Teesdale. It, too, had an Archbishop (Newcome), a Lord Chief Justice (Holt), antiquarians Godwin and Morant, a dazzling linguist, Holwick, and a middling author, Graves.

Wantage had a small Free Grammar School from 1596, though it can only claim a near miss as Archbishop in Bishop Butler, who settled for Chichester instead. Newbury had a very small Free School, so did Uffington, founded in 1638, which is probably where Thomas Hughes started, though he was transferred to Rugby, under the great Dr Arnold. This was part of the trend for separating the education of gentlemen's sons from that of the local farmers and tradesmen's boys. The Grammar Schools were free, at least partly, but these new schools were wholly commercial and attracted boys from all over the country.

Berkshire had its share of the new public schools. Radley College was launched in 1847 by Dr Sewell, who was a member of the Oxford Movement and found a number of parents willing to support him with grants. The money was expended, not only in providing the usual school equipment, but in buying antique furniture, fine paintings and a magnificent organ, costing £1000. A Tibetan carpet was used as bathmat, until someone discovered it was worth £700. Predictably, the school fell in debt to the tune of £40,000 in a decade or so, but was rescued by Lord Addington, who sold many of the antiques and reorganised things in a more practical way, after which it prospered.

Bradfield was founded in 1850 by the wealthy rector, Thomas Stevens, and lavishly equipped (a marked contrast to his views on what was adequate for the poor of the day). Before he died, he had lost his estate and his rectory too was sequestrated, and the school almost foundered. Dr Gray, headmaster in 1880, rescued it, and one of his great achievements was the building (helped by the boys) of a Greek Theatre in a chalk pit in the grounds, which attained more than local fame.

Both these schools were closely connected with the Church of England. The third school built, Wellington College, had another faith entirely—the Army. It was built in 1859 as a memorial to the Duke of Wellington, intended for Army officers' sons (with special provision for the sons of the fallen) and they grew up surrounded by cannons and mementoes of war, close to the Royal Military College at Sandhurst. Oddly enough though, it was Wellington which provided a spring-board to eminence in the church. The first headmaster, Edward White Benson, became Archbishop of Canterbury; the second,

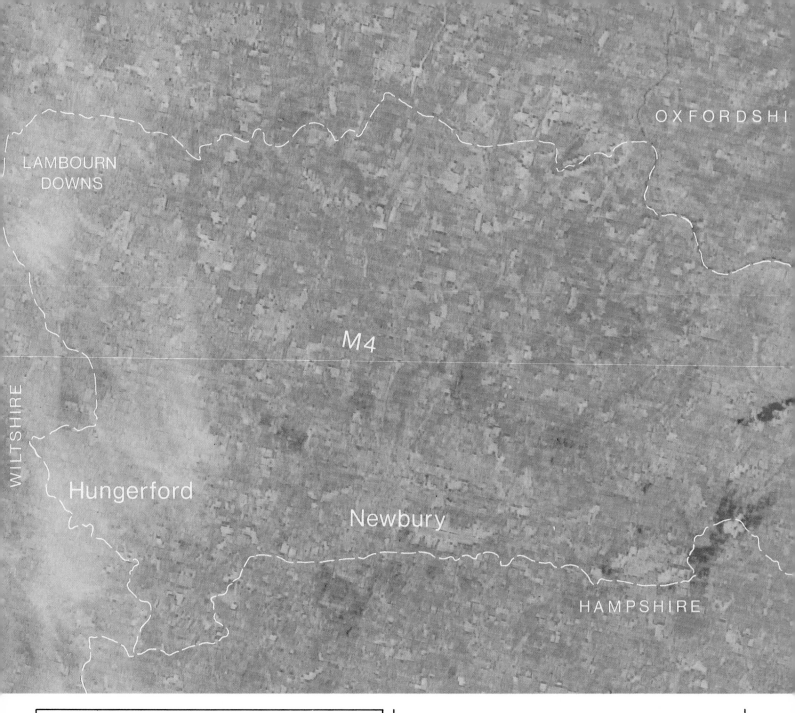

Berkshire satellite image map

This map was made with a Landsat satellite image. It shows the major features: towns, airports, motorways, woods, lakes and rivers.

The image was taken on the 8th June 1976; it was a sunny summer morning in the 'drought' year. There was some thin cloud over Lambourne downs and Hungerford. The satellite was in orbit 915 km above Berkshire. It recorded the land's reflected radiation with four separate cameras, each one recording one of four colours of the spectrum. Three of these wave-band images are combined together photographically to make a colour composite like this one.

The three bands used here are green, red and near infra red. The infra red band is just beyond the sensitivity of the human eye, but it is not thermal or emitted radiation. The image data recorded by the cameras was transmitted to the Landsat ground receiving station at Fucino, Italy. There are computers there to process the imagery and to produce either negatives from which photographic prints can be made or else to record the digital data for use on other image processing computers.

This was processed on a DIAD image processing system operated by Nigel Press Associates Ltd, Edenbridge, Kent. This computer improves the tonal contrast image geometry and quality and produces the negative.

This image map shows urban areas in pinky colours. The motorway is a pink line which can be seen winding across the county. The bare soil fields are also pink. The pasture and crops show in various shades of light green depending on the crop type. The patches of woodland are olive green. Bramshill forest to the south of Bracknell is very clear. The rivers, lakes and reservoirs are purple. The Thames running along the northern county border and the Staines reservoirs are particularly obvious.

A Landsat satellite was first put into orbit by N.A.S.A., USA in 1972 to promote consistent and repetitive image cover of the Earth's surface for producing maps, interpreting geology and monitoring hydrology and agricultural patterns.

Light Green: Fields
Olive Green: Woodland
Pink: Urban areas and bare fields
Purple: Lakes and rivers

Dr Wickham, a dean, and the third, Dr Pollock, Bishop ot Norwich.

Other private schools in the county include The Oratory, Reading (1859); Leighton Park, Reading (1890); Beaumont College, a Catholic foundation (1861); and Douai School, also

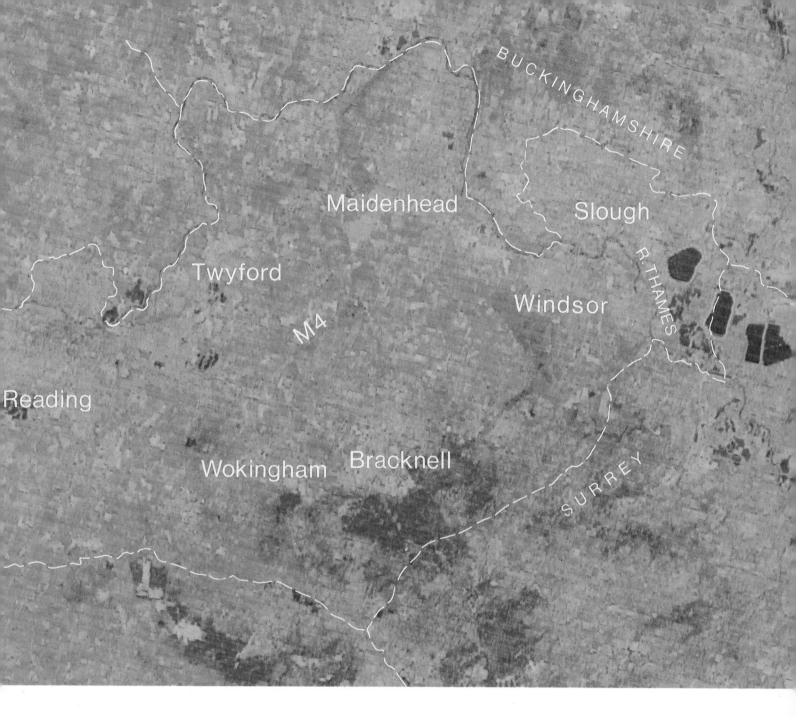

Catholic, founded in France in 1615 and transferred to Woolhampton in 1907. Girls' public schools include St Mary's, Wantage (1873), Downe House, near Newbury (1907) and Abbey School, Reading (1887).

Higher education is catered for by Reading University, founded (as University College) in 1892 with the support of Lord and Lady Wantage, extensive local benefactors, and made up to University status in 1926.

Specialised schools for the armed services are also located in the county. Sandhurst, not far from the enormous camp at Aldershot, is the site of the Royal Military College, moved here from Great Marlow in 1813. Here officer cadets from the British Army, the former Empire and other countries are trained to lead, and every year the best cadet receives a sword of honour from the monarch. Shrivenham, near Faringdon, was selected for the site of a Military College which specialises in technical training and is very handy for the railway works at Swindon. Arborfield is also a centre for the Royal Electrical & Mechanical Engineers.

Rather surprisingly, Berkshire, one of the totally inland counties, is also home for the Pangbourne Nautical College, which trains officers for the Merchant Navy and sometimes for the Marines and Royal Navy. The location was chosen by the Devitt brothers, Sir Thomas and Sir Phillip, who raised the money in 1917.

The Present Day

If the mapmakers of yesteryear and the people whose lives have formed this county history were to return today what would they find most changed? Perhaps the greatest surprise would be the forty-five miles of M4 motorway winding through the countryside like a snake. This has obviously had a radical effect on people's lives and has carved up great tracts of land. On the other hand, it has continued the county's tradition of good communication. Another surprise would surely be Harwell. Where once stood flourishing orchards, fertilised in the seventeenth century by the bodies of people who died in the great plague, now stands the most modern and, in some people's view, the most potentially threatening industry, the Atomic Research Station which has brought high technology to the Thames Valley.

Another shock would be the increasing urbanisation of this agricultural area including Bracknell New Town which has had a major influence on social change since the last war. But not everything would look different. Windsor, which attracts tourists from every corner of the globe, is essentially the same and Lyson's poem still applies:

'Hail Windsor! crowned with lofty towers,
Where nature wantons at her will,
Decks every vale with fruit and flowers,
With waving trees adornes each hill.'

Selected Bibliography

Ashmole, Elias: *History and Antiquities of the County of Berkshire* (1719).

Asser, Michael ed.: *The Royal County: A Berkshire Miscellany to Commemorate the Silver Jubilee of Her Majesty Queen Elizabeth II* (Berkshire County Council, Reading, 1977).

Beresiner, Yasha: *British County Maps. Reference and Price Guide* (Antique Collectors' Club, Woodbridge, Suffolk, 1983).

Berkshire and Reading Committee of the National Register of Archives: *Exhibition of Documents Relating to Berkshire and its Boroughs, 1140–1901* (Reading, 1951).

Booth, John: *Looking at Old Maps* (John Booth, Westbury, Wiltshire, 1979).

Childs, W.M.: *Story of the Town of Reading* (Reading, 1905).

Chubb, Thomas: *The Printed Maps in the Atlases of Great Britain and Ireland 1579–1870* (Dawsons, London, Reprint, 1974).

Coates, C.: *History and Antiquities of Reading* (London, 1802).

Compton, Piers: *The Story of Bisham Abbey* (Maidenhead, 1973).

Deloney, Thomas: *Jack of Newburie* (1597). (Reproduced *Everyman*, 1929).

Deloney, Thomas: *Thomas of Reading or The Six Worthie Yeomen* (1600). (Reproduced *Everyman*, 1929).

Ditchfield, P.H.: *Bygone Berkshire* (Andrews, 1896).

Fletcher, W.: *Reading Past and Present* (Reading, 1839).

Gibbons, A. and Davey, E.C.: *Wantage Past and Present* (William Walter, 1901).

Gray, E.W.: *The History and Antiquities of Newbury and Environs* (Hall and Marsh, 1839).

Higham, Roger: *Berkshire and the Vale of the White Horse* (Batsford, 1977).

Hughes, Thomas: *The Scouring of the White Horse* (Macmillan, 1889).

Hughes, Thomas: *Tom Brown's Schooldays* (London, 1857).

Hull, Felix: *Guide to the Berkshire Record Office, Prepared for the County Records Committee* (Reading, 1952).

Jerome, Jerome K.: *Three Men in a Boat* (London, 1889).

Kingsley, David: *Printed Maps of Sussex 1575–1900* (Sussex Record Society, Lewes, Sussex, 1982). This has detailed information relevant to maps of all the counties.

Lyon, W.: *Chronicles of Finchampstead* (Longmans, 1895).

Monastic Chronicles Consulted:
Anglo-Saxon Chronicle
Asser: *Life of Alfred*
Ingulph: *Chronicle*
Paris, Matthew: *Chronicle*
Richard of Cirencester: *Chronicle*
Roger of Wendover: *History*

Money, W.: *The First and Second Battles of Newbury and the Siege of Donnington Castle* (Simpkins, 1884).

Parkes, Roger: *Alice Ray Morton's Cookham* (Buckingham, 1981).

Ritchie, L.: *Windsor Castle and its Environs* (Longmans, 1840).

Roberts, Cecil: *And so to Bath* (Hodder and Stoughton, 1940).

Smith, David: *Antique Maps of the British Isles* (B.T. Batsford, Ltd, London, 1982).

Stenton, F.M.: *Early History of the British Isles* (Reading, 1913).

Summers, W.H.: *The Story of Hungerford* (London, 1926).

Victoria County History of Berkshire, 4 vols. (London, 1906).

Vincent, J.E.: *Highways and Byways in Berkshire* (Macmillan, 1831).

Williams, A.: *Villages of the White Horse* (Duckworth, 1913).

Yarrow, Ian: *Berkshire* (London, 1973).

Acknowledgements

My grateful thanks are due to Tessa Campbell, Picture Research Editor of *The Map Collector* for her work on the captions and John Freeman for photography.

Information about the authors

Valerie Scott is the editor of a quarterly journal called *The Map Collector* which is read by early map enthusiasts all over the world. She trained as a journalist and worked for newspapers and periodicals before starting *The Map Collector* in December 1977. She lives with her three teenage children on the Buckinghamshire/Hertfordshire border and holds the International Map Collectors Society award for being responsible for the "cartographical contribution of greatest merit and widest interest to map collectors worldwide".

Eve McLaughlin is a professional genealogist and historian who has been covering these subjects for thirty-three years. She researches family trees for clients all over the world, especially Australians and Americans. In addition to providing the family tree she gives the historical background of place and time in which the ancestors lived. Eve is secretary of the Bucks Family History Society and author of the series *McLaughlin Guides for Family Historians*. She lives at Haddenham in Buckinghamshire and has four children.

Isambard Kingdom Brunel's railway line from London to Bristol is recorded in John C. Bourne's The History and Description of the Great Western Railway, 1846. *The scene at Pangbourne illustrates the activity at a "minor station". The text explains that the stations were particularly large and comfortable to accommodate first class passengers—many of whom had their own private carriages and horse boxes for use on the line. (By courtesy of the British Library)*

Families of note in Berkshire

Berkshire families

Baronial

Despencer
D'Oyley
Montacute (E. of Salisbury)
Norreys
Neville (E. of Warwick)
Talbot of Kingston Lisle
Windsor

Medieval Gentry

Abberbury of Donnington
A(r)chard of Sparsholt
Babham
Barbour of Abingdon
de la Beche of Aldworth
Bessils of Besselsleigh
Blacknall of Abingdon
Chaucer
Curzon of Lockinge
Englefield
Estbury
Eyston of East Hendred
Faringdon
Fettiplace
Fitzwilliam of Wantage
Fitwarine of Eastbury
Foxley
de Golafre
Hyde of Denchworth
Litcott
Norris of Wytham
Pleydell of Coleshill
Pocock of Hampstead Norris
Reade of Barton
Pusey
Sparsholt
Walrond

Forster of Aldermaston
Fuller
Gifford of Moulsford
Goddard of Bray
Goodlake of Letcombe Regis
Griffith of Padworth
Gunter of Kintbury
Hartley of Bucklebury
Head of Langley
Mercy of Crutchfield
Hoby of Bisham
Holcot of Barcot
Hopkins of Tidmarsh
Hunter of Mortimer
Hynde of Finchampstead
James of Denford
Keates
Kent of Reading
Lenthall of Besselsleigh
Latton of Blewbury & Chilton
Loder of Hinton Waldrist
Lovelace of Hurley
Lydford of Stanford Dingley
Marten of Kingston Lisle
Mason of Abingdon
Michell of Windsor
Mills of Wadley
Monck of Reading
Newman of Brightwalton
Newberry
Paulet (M. of Winchester)
Palmer of Holme Park
Packer of Bucklebury
Perkins of Ufton Nervet
Pye of Faringdon
Pottinger
Ramsden
Shute (Ld Barrington)
Stonhouse of Radley
Tesdale of Stanford Dingley
Trumbull of Easthampstead
Tull of Basildon
Unton of Wadley
Vansittart of Shottesbrooke
Walter of Bearwood
Ward of Hurst
Wellesbourne of Hanney
Wildman of Shrivenham
Wilmott of Wantage
Wood of Tidmarsh
Yate of Buckland
Young of Cookham

Tudor to the Nabobs

Aldworth of Stanlake
Atkins of Kingston Lisle
Ayshcombe of Hanney
Ball of Arborfield
Barker of Hurst and Stanlake
Barrett of Milton
Blagrave of Watchfield
Blandy (-Jenkins) of
    Kingston Bagpuize
Benyon of Englefield
Bullock of Arborfield
Burgess of Burville
Butler of Inkpen
Castillion
Cherry of Shottesbrooke
Chislett of Sandhurst
Clarke of Aldworth
Clerk of Basildon
Dolman of Shaw
Daunce of Blewbury
Dunch of L. Wittenham
Dundas of Barton
Elwes of Marcham
Essex of Lambourn
Eyre of Welford

Berks Gentry Families in Victorian times

(Martin-) Atkins of
    Kingston Lisle
Best of Donnington
Burton of Childrey
Bouverie -Pusey of Pusey
Bowles of Milton
Clayton -East of Hall Place
Cobham of Shinfield Grange
Croft of Greenham Lodge
Darby-Griffiths of Padworth
Duffield of Marcham
Eyre of Shaw Grange

Gray of Farley Hill Place
Hall-Say of Oakley
Hartley-Russell of Donnington
Hargreaves of Arborfield
Hippisley of Lambourn
Kinnersley of Binfield
Hughes of Uffington
Loyd-Lindsay (Lord Wantage)
Stevens of Bradfield
Vansittart-Neale of Bisham
Vernon of Aldworth
Wilder of Sulham

Some old Berkshire families

Absalom	Clements	Mallam	Trulock
Akers	Clifford	Mattingly	Tubb
Akerman	Copelin	May	Tull
Adams	Copeland	Miles	Watts
Agar	Cordery	Moss	Wellman
Alberry	Cotterell	Nalder	Whitehorn
Aldridge	Coxhead	Nash	Wheeler
Alexander	Daniels	Neale	Wickens
Allum	Darling	Nethercliff	Wither
Allnutt	Eustace	Nightingale	Winterborne
Allwright	Evans	Paine	Wiltshire
Angell	Fisher	Palmer	Wyatt
Appleby	Ford	Paty	Yates
Appleton	Franklin	Pearce	Young
Arlott	Fuller	Pike	
Attwell	George	Pinnell	
Aubrey	Garlick	Pither	
Ayres	Giles	Pocock	
Beckingham	Goodchild	Pottinger	
Beasley	Greenaway	Pound	
Bellchamber	Griffin	Povey	
Bellcher	Grove	Prater	
Benham	Hamblin	Prince	
Best	Harding	Quelch	
Biddle	Hatt	Rance	
Bint	Hazell	Randall	
Bitmead	Holder	Rivers	
Blackman	Hunt	Sadler	
Blake	Hussey	Seymour	
Blay	James	Sherwood	
Blissett	Jennings	Shorter	
Bond	Jones	Simmonds	
Bonny	Keep	Smallbone	
Boote	Kent	Southby	
Bowyer	King	Spanswick	
Bradfield	Knapp	Spinage	
Brant	Lamborne	Spindlow	
Bristow	Leaver	Streak	
Berrker	Lewington	Stroud	
Buckner	Loder	Swain	
Bunce	Looker	Thatcher	
Cannon	Lovegrove	Tilling	
Castle	Lovelock	Titcomb	
Chamberlain	Mackrell	Tovey	
Childs	Major	Trayhorn	

☒ Knight Frank & Rutley

The Knight Frank & Rutley Group, which is glad to be associated with this book, comprises nine autonomous firms operating through twenty-nine offices in Western Europe, West and Central Southern Africa, North America and the Far East. They have common standards of professionalism and a common aim to provide the best possible service for clients of the Group, no matter in which country the interests may originate.

Quiller Press Ltd., 50 Albemarle Street,
London W1X 4BD.

First Published 1984

Copyright © 1984 text: Valerie G. Scott
and Eve McLaughlin

ISBN 0 907621 33 3

Designed by Brian Lock
Design and production in association
with Book Production Consultants, Cambridge
Printed by The Burlington Press, Foxton, Herts.